Embrace Ultra Ability!

Wisdom, Insight & Motivation from the Blind Who Sees Far and Wide

Shirley Cheng

www.DanceWithYourHeart.com

Wappingers Falls, New York

Copyright © 2008 by Shirley Cheng

ISBN: 978-0-6151-5522-7
Library of Congress Control Number: 2007906292

www.DanceWithYourHeart.com
Wappingers Falls, New York, United States of America

Cover © Photographer: Eric Gevaert
Agency: Dreamstime.com

All rights reserved by the author, Shirley Cheng. No part of this publication may be reproduced, stored in a retrieval system, or transmitted in any form or by any means, electronic, mechanical, photocopying, recording or otherwise, without the prior written permission of Shirley Cheng.

Nine-Time Winner
Parent to Parent Adding Wisdom Award
Finalist
National Best Books 2008 Awards

&

2008 Next Generation Indie Book Awards

With all my heart and soul, I dedicate this book to the greatest present God has ever bestowed upon me: my beloved and spiritually strong mother Juliet Cheng, who is a main reason why I am not disabled but ultra-abled. I love you, Mom!

Table of Contents

Embrace Jehovah 7
A Matter of Time 14
One Step at a Time 16
It's Your Present! 18
Are You a Friend of Time Wasters? 19
What If You Think Without Ifs? 25
How Real Is It? 28
Learn How to Learn 31
Follow the Light 36
The Tree of Spiritual Success 41
Always a Tomorrow 61
Are You Happy? 69
Branches of Spiritual Success 73
The Brave Bringer of Life 79
Love the Life You Live 84
The Power of Positivity 97
The Null of Negativity 99
Rise and Overcome! 103
Be Logically Sensitive, Stay Emotionless 109
Through Maternal Love, Justice Prevails 113
What's in It for Me? 124
Are You Hungry Enough? 126
Go for Your Gold Medals in Life! 128
How Daring Are You? 134
Disable Your Disability 138
Acceptance or Rejection? 141
Win with Positivity 144
Last Few Words 150
Spotlight Reviews 152
About the Author 160

Embrace Jehovah

When you look out your window, what do you see? I remember seeing the green foliage of trees, their greenness shimmering under the loving, ardent kiss of the sun, and how the leaves danced when the winds whistled through them. I remember admiring the birds hovering overhead and swanning so gracefully. I have very fond memories of these lovely scenes of nature, of life. Without my eyesight, I continue to enjoy life as I savor every sound I hear, every fragrance I smell, and every exquisite touch of something soft or delicate.

Feeling life through my senses, I am in awe of it all. How is that everything and everyone, from the tiniest atoms to the shooting stars, is in existence and has come into existence, without having been created? How could such a complex universe possibly be so surprisingly harmonic and exist in such seamless order if existing on its own? Look around you—the skies, the trees, the mountains, the flora and fauna—are they not awe inspiring? Or simply take a look at the front cover of this book. Is this scene of nature not stunningly breathtaking, magnificent, powerful, mysterious, and fantastic? Could you deny the existence of a Creator when you look at it? No, there has to be a power that created all these beauties, these miracles. This power is the one and only God Almighty.

God is everything. He is all virtues: Love, Wisdom, Righteousness, Mercy, and Forgiveness. He is the Creator of everything in the universe, all that is visible and invisible; all that is audible and inaudible; all that can be felt, tasted, and smelled; and the intangible and ethereal. Everything is a part of Him. He is infinite, total, and all encompassing. He has existed since before the beginning of time. He has no beginning nor has He any end. And His name is Jehovah.

Jehovah is the working force behind everything and every order: He aids you in your every achievement; He is absent during your every fall. Without Jehovah, neither your life nor life's virtues will exist.

Life is beautiful, a sheer work of love. God created life with love. But how could there be darkness and pain when God has used pure love to create everything? Why are there innocent people suffering, starving, tortured, abused, and homeless? Why do some people's lives end before they had a chance to begin, such as in stillbirths? The answers lie in the Bible, so if one carefully studies it with one's heart, the truth will be found. Currently, our world is ruled by the "father of lies," whose reign has brought misery and death upon Earth. But his rulership of this system of things will not last very long, as one righteous King will soon look after us for eternity. Thus, for the time being, the purpose of life is to 1) learn, fulfill, and pass on the Word of God and His divine teachings; 2) be a good person with good intentions; and 3) enjoy life to its fullest, enjoy all that life has to offer. It is our duty in life to be good and to do good; that is the most important aspect of life. Once you achieve goodness, you will accept your purpose more easily. Above all, you will be ready to embrace a new life of light and love forever.

If you have the strong desire and the willingness to be gently guided on the right path to life, read this book. If you are truly serious and dedicated to being a good person in every way possible, then let your soul welcome new insights and inspiration to embrace goodness.

True empowerment starts in oneself. Nothing and nobody can change your views. Not even God will change your views—He does not have the desire to change your views, even though He has the power to do so. He gives you all your skills and talents, but He does not control your heart. He sees everything in one's heart, and lets everyone develop his or her heart on his or her own. Jehovah gives us the free will to decide for ourselves. He sets us free, without brainwashing our minds. He allows us to do what we want, to establish our rules and laws; he does not control our thoughts, feelings, and actions. He gives you the freedom to use His gifts however you wish; all that He asks from us is to use His gifts wisely. He informs us of the consequences if we go against His wishes. Only you have the power to change your life around, with plenty of help from God.

This small book is simply a tender nudge, a support for you on your path to greatness. Remember that God has provided everyone all the resources to be truly successful individuals, and we just have to know how to accept and use them to our best ability. Just as school teachers provide students with formulas and examples to learn, God has supplied us with all the necessary tools to live, and it is our duty as students to follow them and utilize them wisely.

Jehovah's resources are precious, the blueprints to a happy life, but many times, people overlook their values and put them aside. I am a lucky soul who has accepted His gems from the start, and I continually acquire more as I journey down my life's road. Here, I wish to share with you how truly wonderful these treasures are, so you will be able to experience all that pure life has to offer. I am too small a person to keep them all to myself, so I invite you to hold my hand as we learn and experience together.

When you have accepted God and all the virtues He supplies, you will become ultra-abled. If you use His treasures with love, care, and wisdom, you will become ultra-abled. If a wealthy man gave you a sack of precious gemstones, but you did not realize their value and how to use them, what good would they do you? You have the power to disable yourself or enable yourself, so which road would you choose? I have chosen to be ultra-abled, for I am a treasure collector: I pick up the gems God graciously gives in full abundance. With these gifts, I am able to make choices in my life that could lead me to the road of happiness, strength, and success.

This book is simply a guide and should not be used as your primary source. God is the one and only primary resource; His Bible is the first and most important resource you need in order to find guidance and life's knowledge. Seek God in your heart and He shall give you all truths and knowledge you crave. Accept Him as your savior and beacon and you will know that you are not alone.

The ascertaining of knowledge starts here—we have to start somewhere—and this is our first step. In time, we will understand much more, if not everything.

I do not do anything special, nor am I any more special than anyone else living or dead. I am simply one who has accepted God into my heart to learn from Him, to receive knowledge from Him. I may be wise, but it is the wisdom that He gives me to pursue more wisdom. I may be happy, but it is the happiness that He gives me to pursue more happiness. He provides the fuel, the ingredients, for me to move forward and to collect more treasures as I happily journey down my life's road.

We all live and learn. I believe life is a giant school. Jehovah has a purpose much greater than we all can imagine, and He will soon fulfill that wonderful plan. Our lives on this planet are just a beginning. The real world awaits us after this system, so we must prepare for whatever lies ahead.

My book covers the fundamental aspects of life: values and virtues, the essential ingredients people's decisions are based upon. Just as a house needs a good and strong foundation to withstand the elements of time and nature, you need a sturdy foundation in order to live a good life and to make the right decisions. And just as we need water and nutrients to survive, we need a spiritual foundation to live a meaningful life. It is up to you to create your foundation and keep it strong and invincible. I suggest a strong foundation for the sake of goodness, for the sake of true happiness in your life right now, and to live with harmony not only for yourself but for others as well. It is never too late to build your foundation. Build it as early as possible, so you can use it as soon and as much as you can. All you need is the desire and the willingness to create your foundation. I cannot put the desire into you; only you have the power to fire your own soul. When you are ready, when your heart is open and relaxed, begin building your foundation by turning to the next page.

I wish you the best in life and all that you do. When you have built your foundation, be ready to welcome joy into your heart and love life like never before! Embrace Jehovah and His gifts and you will embrace ultra-ability!

A Matter of Time

How would you like to have the power to see into the future? For many, at first thought, that is a power they would crave. Truthfully, if I do not give it some thought, I would say that I would love to have the power to see into the future, to know what will happen next and whom I will meet. However, after carefully considering it, I prefer to keep the future a secret instead. I like the moments when life throws me surprises, and I have received plenty of them, both good and bad. Just as I do not read the last few pages of a book to find out the ending, I would not want to live a life without any excitement, without knowing how and why I got to the place I have gotten myself.

Life likes to shout "Surprise!" when we least expect it. Thus, we have to use every bit of our time to cross our fingers and wish for the best. While we hope for a bright tomorrow, we need to capture our time right now before it slips away between the cracks of everyday rushes.

The best way to capture time is to cherish every minute of your existence. Value every step you take. Take your time with life. If you rush through life, you are merely speeding to your grave. What is the hurry? Everyone acts as though they must finish their job as soon as possible. When you are on medication, you take one dose at a time. Taking the entire bottle at once will not give you a speedy recovery. By wanting everything to move faster, you are wishing away time, and thus you will be gone before you have enough time to realize it. So be patient and take life one step at a time. Do not rush to your grave. You have only one life on Earth, so make the most of it. Hold on to the happy memories you and your loved ones build together.

Time is precious. If you do not pay attention to it, it will fly away, and then it will be too late. Time is a natural resource that can be used up, so use it wisely when you can. Do not wait to do the things that are important to you. If you want to spend time with your friends and family, do it now, not later. Later may be too late. Do not let time run out.

Many times, we are excited about an important event in our lives—a graduation, a party, a wedding—and we wish that it would arrive soon. I remember looking forward to my seventeenth birthday party. After I turned seventeen, I lost my eyesight. We do not know what tomorrow will bring, so hold on to today when you can, and cherish your present.

One Step at a Time

We primarily have three stages or phases in our lives, and each stage is as unique and different, and yet the same, as the others. They are our past, present, and future. Each period is connected with one another. Tomorrow will be our present the next day, and our present will become our past tomorrow. So each stage is as important as any other stage. In order to impact your past and future in a positive way, you need to focus on your present. Devote your energy to one stage of your life at a time.

The past is a part of your life; why should you forget what you have experienced, felt, and learned? The past should not be a blur. Otherwise, what you learn today will all become a waste tomorrow. Yet many people use their past as a ground for remorse, rather than as reflection. They tend to dwell on the past, regretting the things they did, and, above all, the things they did not do. They wish they could turn back time to make another decision, to change the route they took. But the past is the past. You cannot change your past, so why dwell on it? It may be true that you have made some really dumb decisions in the past—marrying the wrong person or cheating on your spouse—and those choices may have affected your life in a negative and lasting way, but because you do not have the power to turn back time, all you can do now is do your best with the present. The only fix to a mistake you have made is to move forward.

By moving forward in life, you can change your life around. That does not mean you can resolve every problem. What it does mean is that you will be able to live a better life. Your past is the part of life from which you can learn. Once you have realized that you have made a mistake, you can learn not to make the same mistake again. If you regret cheating on your spouse, then never do that again.

Your future will be based on the decisions you make today, so choose to do things wisely right now. Focus your energy, time, and effort entirely on your present in order to establish a bright future.

It's Your Present!

What is wrong with the below sentence? (No, this is not a grammar quiz!)

"Live each day as though it is your last."

People say this to one another to urge others to live life to its fullest. It may seem encouraging, but there is always something about this "encouragement" I do not quite like. So I decided to refurbish that sentence a bit. Now how does the new sentence sound?

"Do not live each day as though it is your last; live each day as though it is your first!"

Does that sound much better?

You had probably never realized that "living each day as though it is your last" is really a negative idea.

Live your life in such a way that each day is a new experience for you. Just like a child receiving a brand-new present, you are experiencing the present for the first time; life is the gift from God. Use your present to explore and make new discoveries.

Death is inevitable, but why let it hover over your head like a dark cloud? Why live each day as though you are going to die tomorrow? Subtract the negativity!

Enjoy your new day!

Are You a Friend of Time Wasters?

We all know that time is a precious resource. (You do, do you not?) But quite often, our actions do not match our beliefs and thoughts on the matter. We do things that waste our time while putting what we should do way behind us — right at the back of our minds. Sure, you need to relax and not work all the time, but I am referring to the activities you often automatically do without giving much thought to them. Relaxing and meditating are productive; smoking, gambling, and sitting in front of your television set for an extended period of time are not. I will briefly touch upon the most common time wasters we encounter, some of them you may never have realized as such.

Smoking is a huge time waster. All you can do while you are smoking is, well, smoke — unless you are one who does deep thinking about life's issues during smoking. Not only is smoking wasting your precious time, it is costly to both your pocket and your health, most especially the latter.

Gambling could be fun if it is not done excessively and especially if it does not involve money, but that is rarely the case. Thus, gambling is a definite no-no. It is an extremely expensive time waster. It is an activity that can potentially cost you everything. Many people sell their belongings and go through heavy debt and financial burdens and troubles as a result of excessive gambling.

We know what drinking too much can do to you. Social drinking is acceptable, but many people become aggressive and do silly or dangerous things on impulse when too much alcohol gets into their system.

As for watching too much television—quite a few people have been guilty of it, but I am glad to say that I am not one of them. Watching one or two hours of television is perfectly fine, especially if the content is educational or entertaining without corrupting your mind. Television viewers are exposed to so much inappropriate content nowadays, content that young audiences take to be the norm (sadly, much of what is portrayed on television has indeed become the norm in our society) and come to believe is acceptable, including murdering and raping their peers. Television watching used to be a safe source of education and entertainment. Now parents have to guard what their children see. Sitting on your couch in front of your television, with a bag of popcorn (it may be your third serving) is not only wasting your time but also stuffing your mind and tummy with valueless fillers.

There are plenty of other time wasters that will do you harm if they are done excessively. Paying too much attention to your outward appearance not only wastes your time, but also wastes your true self. We are the way we are born, but unfortunately, not everyone can accept who they are. Instead, they hide themselves under false coloring and heavy makeup, and some go to the extreme of having plastic surgery and receiving implants that are risky to their health, not to mention their bank accounts. Why is it so hard to accept the way we are? Why can we not realize that what truly count are the values we hold inside? It is easy for people to become beautiful paper roses, but what good is that when it does not hold any inner worth? It is not easy to become a real rose, blossoming beauty from the inside, but that should be our ultimate goal. While I do not have anything against fixing oneself up a bit to look presentable, being fake and artificial is not admirable. Everyone wears different clothing, some with floral designs, some with stripes, and others in solid colors. Just as you should not judge someone by what they wear, you should not judge someone by their natural outward appearance. How we naturally look is the clothing we are born in. Accept the clothes life supplies you. Always value the inner beauty you and others possess. If other people cannot accept the true you, and instead judge you by your appearance, then too bad for them!

Speaking of being fake, fake gentility is another of those things that wastes your time. You might not have thought of it that way, but think about it: everything you do uses precious time, so pretending to be someone you are not is no exception. Pretense is void; it holds no value in itself, and someone who lives with pretense lives with no meaning. It is not the same when you grit your teeth to be polite to someone you do not quite like. Fake gentility is pretending to be a different person all the time in front of many people. You are, in essence, living someone else's life, not your own.

That brings us to the activity of showing off. As with fake gentility, it wastes your time because you perform an empty task. Being arrogant and snobby also falls under this category.

Worry can be harmful when every second counts. You are letting time slip away when you fret over anything. For every second you spend worrying, you waste time that could have been spent productively thinking about and analyzing your problem. The more often you worry, the more worried you will become. Worrying is endless—you can worry about anything and everything until you pass away. It is best to stop your worrying now rather than having your death stop it for you.

Spreading rumors throws away your time as well. Although chitchatting with your friends is fun and memorable, spreading untruths is not a wise way to live your life.

Complaining is yet another automatic time waster. Does complaining fix whatever you complain about? It is fine to get whatever is bothering you off your chest, but complaining and being upset and angry about something over an extensive period not only wastes your time but also is not good to your mental health and spirit. There are complainers who complain to get other people's attention or sympathy. The worst kind of complainers take it a step further: they complain about people who are truly good to them, including family members, to receive sympathy from strangers or outsiders. Their complaints are mostly peppered with lies, for who could honestly find anything to complain about when there is nothing to find fault with in the first place? As a result, they waste time in many ways: complaining, lying, and betraying the trust and love of the good and true.

Fighting and bickering can be the same as being angry or upset, but with a much worse physical and mental effect. Violence, either done verbally or physically — especially the latter — is never a way to successfully resolve a problem.

We measure time by calculating what we have achieved. When you waste your time in the ways I have mentioned here, you have spent a lot of time, but put none of it to good use.

So how do you know that you are not doing something that wastes your time? To find out, ask yourself the following questions:

1. Am I learning something? Learning is not just about book material; you can learn about a life matter or gain a new perspective on an issue. So if you spend five hours on a computer, and most of that time, you are

learning something, then you are not wasting your time.

2. Is what I am doing morally acceptable? It is important to use your time to be a good person; time spent on goodness is the most worthwhile time ever spent. Doing something immoral wastes away your value. You may think, "How could what I am doing be unacceptable when everyone else I know does it?" Does that make the activity morally acceptable? Just because many people do the same thing does not mean what they do is morally right.

3. How do I feel after performing the activity? Do I feel spiritually cleared and rejuvenated? Am I happier and more relaxed? Do I feel content after the task? Do I feel truly good about myself afterward? If your activities make you feel in some way empty or uneasy, you have not spent your time wisely. This is especially true if you feel ashamed or embarrassed to tell others what you did.

The reason some people are good friends with time wasters is because they do not realize the importance and value of every minute. In essence, they do not understand the importance and value of life. When you truly want to live a worthwhile life, you will be able to know how to identify time wasters, and thus, never let them take up your time.

So be a lover of life and scorn those time wasters!

What If You Think Without Ifs?

When you think about the past, stay away from *if* and *what if*. *If*, although a tiny word, is a huge trouble maker. It brings you to a never-ending and fruitless quest: *If I had said no… If I had driven slower… What if I went home earlier?* One *if* question will lead to another, wasting away your energy and leaving you frustrated and hopeless. *If* thoughts will supply you with only vain answers. By answering your *if* questions, you may be comforted by speculating a better outcome of your past decisions, but what good will that do you in the present? You cannot change your past no matter how many *ifs* and *what ifs* run through your head, so the best thing to do is never think with *if*, unless it teaches you a lesson. For instance, "If I had not eaten too much of that ice cream with milk, I would not have gotten this bad case of stomach ache," will tell you to avoid doing the same thing next time.

For me, if I had not received that tuberculin skin test when I was eleven months old, I would not have contracted juvenile rheumatoid arthritis. But what was done was done and could not be undone. Life has too many different roads for us to choose from, each with a door that has *If* written on it. Many times, we can open only one of the doors at every crossroad we come to and hope for the best. Once you have opened a door, move forward and do not look back to the other *if* doors. They have passed.

What about the present and future? Is it feasible to think about *if*? You can certainly think about all the possibilities to a situation with *if* questions, but do not overthink them, for it will simply glue you to one spot and will be as much as a trouble maker for you as it is when dealing with the past. It is wise to think about the pros and cons of the decisions you make, and then pick one desired possible outcome. Note the word "possible." We can not predict what outcomes we will receive, not even if we spend hours analyzing the *ifs*. "If I go out with this person, I will be happy," may or may not be so. The best way to find out the answer to an *if* question is do it and see what it will bring.

Just as with *if* questions for the past, *if* questions for the future can be as torturous. *If I begin a new job, I may not be good at it. If I am not good at it, people will laugh behind my back. If people laugh at me, I will be so embarrassed. If I get embarrassed, I...* You get the idea. True, that line of questions started with a negative *if* question, which is the kind most of us unconsciously choose; that is how we think when we are worried about the future. Positive *if* questions, although more, well, positive, also lead to vain speculations. *If I become an author, I will become famous. If I become famous, I will become rich. If I am rich, I will buy a multi-million-dollar mansion…* But you can put this way of thinking to good use if you turn your positive *if* questions into your goals, but do not count on your possible outcomes. If you become an author, you may not be famous, but you can certainly make that dream come true, with plenty of passion and faith.

What if you think without ifs for a change? What do you think that will do for you? Try it and find out for yourself.

How Real Is It?

Hairy black tarantulas are the scariest creatures you have ever known. You think they are the creepiest beasts that have ever walked on the planet, and you honestly do not know why God would create such beastly critters. That is how you see tarantulas (come on, just pretend you do anyway). Well, your friend thinks you are crazy. He absolutely adores tarantulas. As a matter of fact, he has a pet tarantula named Henry, whom he pets with loving strokes. So whose reality of tarantulas is correct? Are they really that awful, or are they actually adorable?

The answer is that neither reality is accurate for everyone, but each is true for the person it concerns. You determine your own reality. You create your reality by listening to how your heart feels. Your conscience's perception creates your reality. For instance, in my situation, I am both blind and physically disabled, and yet, I am still a very happy person. I feel happiness in my heart, which dances, and I dance along with it. So my reality is that I am a happy person despite my blindness and disabilities. But my reality may not be someone else's reality. A stranger will see that I am a blind person with physical disabilities, and his heart will feel that I may be an unhappy person. In his reality, being blind and disabled is a good reason for being unhappy, or at least, not being happy.

Since everyone's reality in a given situation can vary greatly, your opinion is the most important opinion in your life, including your opinion of yourself. People can say how great you are, but if you do not believe it, it will not do you any good. On the other hand, if people say negative things about you, but you know they are not true, you will still feel good about yourself.

Let me stress again that your opinion is the most important opinion. If you truly believe you have progressed in life when others disagree, you will still be satisfied. If you do not feel that you have progressed, even if others say otherwise, your progress will not mean much to you. If you know you cannot do something, you are right; if you believe you can do something, you are right also. If you believe your life is full, it *is* full, no matter what other people say.

People's values, beliefs, standards, opinions, likes, and dislikes, are all different. So it is wise to listen to how you feel. After all, it is your life; you have the right to live it however you like based on your own principles, as long as those principles are good and sound.

Other people's opinions should not count. How can they count when every person gives you a different opinion? However, if many people give you the same opinion, there may be a good reason to listen to them if you desire. But how do you know to whose opinion you should listen? Whose advice should you take? How would you know who is right?

If you do not know whose opinion to accept and take seriously, ask yourself who truly cares and loves you and whom you honestly trust. Those are the people to whom you can listen. Those who are good and respected in the society might also be people you could trust.

Lastly, compare other people's opinions with your own values. Just because many people tell you the same thing does not necessarily mean that their opinions are sound or morally acceptable. Just because many people do the same thing does not mean what they do is ethical. So your own value system is essential in helping you decide to whom to listen. To read more about values, turn to the chapter in this book titled "The Tree of Spiritual Success" found on page forty-one.

Do not completely depend on other people's words; you need to have your own values, beliefs, and ideas by which to live. Otherwise, you will simply be tossed around like a volleyball. Above all, establishing your own ideas is vital in order to properly care for others around you, such as your children. If you need guidance in establishing your values, seek God's Word. Who else could give you better guidance and support than your own Creator?

Learn How to Learn

Historians research and write down everything that went right and everything that went wrong in our past. We take history classes to see what went right or wrong, and why events happened the way they did, so we can learn how not to repeat the same mistakes, errors, and offenses. We live and learn, and we can learn from the past and the errors people made, so we can live a better present.

It is important to learn from your past without dwelling on it. Life moves on no matter what happens to you, and you have the option to move along with it or be stuck in the hole you created for yourself.

Although life is about learning and living, the trick is to know how to learn. You cannot base your lessons on only one event, and on only causes and effects; it is more than that. You would have to determine the subjects (what and who caused the problem). Then you would have to examine the duration, the setting, and the topic.

The next few pages provide a few examples on how to learn from the past.

Example I

Situation A:

You were in a rocky relationship with Pat. Pat did not like the way you talked, the way you walked, and even how you smelled. So you ended the relationship.

Situation B:

Because of your relationship with Pat, you are doubtful of entering into a relationship with Robin.

What to examine:

Is Situation A the same as Situation B? Do these involve the same people (subjects)? Because you went through a bad relationship in Situation A, you may be afraid to start a new relationship in Situation B. Yet your new partner, Robin, is a totally different person from Pat. Different ingredients, no matter the situation, will produce different effects. Robin may like the way you talk, the way you walk, and even appreciate the fruity perfume you wear.

There are ways to learn from experiences, and one of them is not to learn from one experience, but rather learn from an extended period of time. You have to look at the whole picture, examine every angle, not just what went right and wrong. What were the subjects? Are the subjects different than the ones in the past? Was the situation different? Is it in a variable, dynamic environment? Let us say that you had dated ten people, and most of them negatively commented you on the way you talk, walk, and smell. Obviously, there must be some truth in what they say, so you will need to give their comments some consideration. But if Pat was the only one who did not like how you smell, that may be just one opinion of an individual.

Should you go ahead with the new relationship in Situation B? That is totally up to you. What are your desires and deepest yearnings? Do you desire to find a soul mate? If so, what is holding you back? Is it fear? Is fear of having a bad experience so much more important than your desires? How would you be so certain that you will end up with another bad relationship? Even if you do, you can always end your relationship. But you will never know whether you can find the perfect person if you never try it. To get an answer to something, you have to try it and experience it yourself. What you experience and go through will give you the answer. It may not be the answer you want, but it will be an answer nevertheless. You cannot always get the desirable answer. Sometimes truth hurts, but it is the fact of life, and you simply have to face it.

You have to take chances and risks, and not be afraid of any losses you may experience. What if it goes right? You will never know if you do not try.

Example II

Situation A:
You were telling blond jokes to a group of your friends, but many of the jokes offended your naturally blond friend.

Situation B:
You got together again with the same group of friends, including your naturally blond friend. You refrained from telling blond jokes this time.

In this case, the subjects—you and your naturally blond friend—are the same in both Situation A and Situation B, so it may be a good idea not to tell blond jokes to avoid upsetting your friend. This time, you have learned from the past, and you took precautions. If the situation with the same subjects happened wrong the first time, there is some chance that it will happen again. Yet every case is different. You cannot entirely predict what will happen from the past. You may get an idea about how things may happen, but life progresses—people change, life changes—so you cannot completely base your present and future on the past. Thus, in the second example, you may want to ask your blond friend before deciding whether to tell the jokes. Perhaps your friend has changed his or her opinion on the jokes and now knows not to take them seriously.

Example III

Situation A:
The stock market has been performing well throughout its history. There have been bumps along the way, but the growth has been steady and all that was lost has been more than recovered.

Situation B:
You plan to invest in the stock market, thinking that it is a good investment based on its performance.

Because you are looking at an extended period of time in Situation A, there is a good chance that the market will continue to rise, so going ahead with investing in stocks in Situation B is a good idea. But there have been bumps, and the stock market may experience another bump anytime, so you will have to take precautions with your investments and prepare for any losses.

Follow the Light

To be enlightened, you must seek a light source, rather than a dark source. If you need to search for something in a dark closet, you do not close the door in order to find it. Instead, you turn on the lights in the closet or open the door to use light from an outside source. So if you want to be happy, surround yourself with happy people. If you want to be miserable (which I would find hard to believe), have miserable people as your company. If you want to achieve, follow in the footsteps of achievers, not of failures. If you want to learn to dance, spend time with dancers. If you want to be a writer, join writers' groups, not sports groups, unless you write about sports.

The sources you seek can determine or help lead you in the right direction. You first have to have a good idea where you want to go in life and how you want to feel. If you simply want to be more positive, surround yourself with positive people.

Positive people are strong motivators and role models. When you are with a positive person who can achieve big despite their challenges, you will be able to be motivated. You will have the desire to follow their examples. For instance, I sometimes receive comments from aspiring writers such as, "If you can do it, so can I!" They see that I am still able to become a successful writer despite my blindness and physical disabilities, so in turn, they are motivated to go for their own writing dreams, regardless of whether they are blind or sighted, disabled or abled.

If you want to feel better spiritually, spend time with happy people, those who make others feel good. When you are around someone who has a great sense of humor and tells hilarious jokes all the time, you cannot help but laugh, or at least, smile. On the other hand, when you are around a person who complains and needs you to comfort her, but no matter what you say or do, that person will not cheer up—you will be wasting your energy on just trying to think of ways to console that person. When all of your energy is used up, you are left feeling bad yourself. You will also be complaining. If someone complains all the time and is stuck in their miserable state, not achieving anything while wasting their energy, no one will want to be in their situation.

After you have found the right source to follow, how do you know how to learn from the source? It can be tricky at times to use your source correctly; the method may not be what it appears to be. In most cases, you use your source by comparison.

You need to know the trick to comparison. First, you need to use it in a positive way, not in a negative way. You can tell whether you are using comparison correctly by seeing how you feel afterward. In the following example, when you compare your modest home with that of a wealthy doctor, you may feel either motivated or downcast, depending on how you do the comparison.

Possibility A:
After comparison, you feel less significant.

Possibility B:
You feel motivated to emulate the doctor's success by achieving more in your life.

How can you turn Possibility A into Possibility B?

First, do not feel worthless when you compare what you do not have with what the doctor has—that is, his large house versus your small house. Do not focus on what you do not have—it will only make you feel unhappy.

Second, do not compare the surface or materialistic objects, but rather the intangible values. Although your pockets may hold less value, how would you know that your life itself is worth less than the doctor's? You may see a life gilded in gold, but would you know what is underneath? Do you know if the doctor is truly happy? Does he have a good family and true friends? Admire those who are happy and good, not simply wealthier or healthier. Follow in the footsteps of those who are happier, not of those who are only more successful or wealthier, unless you know the true ingredients to making yourself genuinely happy, not simply wealthy and prominent.

Third, think how the doctor became financially successful. It must have taken him a lot of time and effort to build up the wealth.

Lastly, it is necessary to differentiate between envy and admiration. If you feel ashamed of yourself and resent others after comparing your life with the life of a happier, more successful person, then you are envying that person. On the other hand, if you feel more motivated to follow their example on being happier yourself, then you are appreciating their life but not belittling your life in any way.

In other words, if you feel the least bit frustrated or unhappy, that shows you are using your source the wrong way. On the other hand, if you do not feel the least bit sad or down, you are doing the comparison correctly.

Do not compare your life with those whose lives are more desirable in the sense of materialism. Many times, people take their fortunes for granted. They tend to compare themselves with someone who is richer, prettier, healthier, smarter, or more successful, and never learn from those who are seemingly less fortunate than they are: the blind, the disabled, and the homeless. Yet, many of these people, including yours truly, are able to rise above their challenges and come out as happy, grateful human beings.

Hence, often times, people do not realize

a good source when it is right under their noses. They overlook those who are hidden in the shadows: those who have less in material but much more in value and inner treasures. Learn from the blind with vision, the disabled who can climb high mountains, and the deaf who can listen with their hearts. Spend time with them. See why they are so happy and how you can be as happy as they are.

If all else fails, next time when you feel sorry for yourself, when you feel that your life is not good or that you are not happy about your life, pay a visit to the homeless on the streets, the sickly in the hospitals and nursing homes, and the starved in Africa. How would you like to exchange places with them?

The Tree of Spiritual Success

In life, everything is divided into mainly two categories: the spiritual and the worldly. What belong to the spiritual realm are everlasting. They do not know time; they do not know age. They withstand all trials and tribulations. Those who welcome the spiritual elements will achieve true success and happiness that will last well beyond the life in this world, while leaving a legacy.

The worldly, on the other hand, give you only earthly success: wealth, power, and fame. When you die, they die with you. What good is a roomful of money when you are dead? When we live, we need to collect treasures that will last forever so we can enjoy happiness forever. Many times, we are so focused on achieving what our flesh wants, forgetting that whatever our flesh achieves will die with our flesh.

So being a spiritual person, embracing the spiritual aspects, will lead you to an enduring, fulfilling life. We are here to strengthen our spirits, to learn what Heavenly Father wants from us, so we can return His love and live by His almighty rule, eternally.

This chapter is dedicated to helping you build a spiritual foundation, which will be useful in every aspect of your life. It will aid you in focusing on what you want in life, directing you on the right path to take, and dealing with and overcoming obstacles, from everyday challenges to life's traumas.

This foundation should consist of five principles or virtues. All other principles or elements in life will be derived from these five spiritual ingredients. This is the basic structure, in its most essential form. The shorter the formula, the easier it can be remembered and the more often people can apply it. So it has to be sweet and simple.

Before I go into the five elements, I want you to first picture a tree. I call this tree the Tree of Spiritual Success. The trunk is the foundation of five elements. When you have the foundation planted firmly in the ground, the tree will grow. It will produce many branches, and these branches are the additional desirable elements that come from your foundation. From these branches, more branches will grow, and they will bear fruits. These fruits are the fruits of your labor, the desired end result of your foundation, your achieved goals.

The ingredients that make up the foundation are faith, gratitude, your values, love, and hope.

Faith

Faith is having complete confidence, loyalty, or allegiance to a cause or a person. It is vital to have deep faith in something, someone, or God, in order to live comfortably, with less fear, worry, and doubt.

Think back to when you were a baby. You were born with complete and infinite faith and trust. Your life, all your needs, were in the hand of whoever took care of you.

So as an adult, have steady faith, and trust that you can do it, you can make it. Let life unfold and progress effortlessly. Events in life happen at the right time for the right reason, although we cannot always understand the reasoning behind all events. Just as God has made our bodies to regulate themselves, He has made life to regulate itself. So let it be; let it go. Be carefree.

First and foremost, have unwavering and all-encompassing faith in God. Just as you had deep faith in your parents or guardian when you were a helpless infant, have faith in our Heavenly Father. After all, He is our Creator, and we are His children. Does it not make some sense that we trust in Him?

Personally, I have this deep faith in God to get me through the toughest times. I put all my trust, all my hopes, all my dreams, in His hands. I let Him take care of my problems as I enjoy life. I am a sheep in his green pasture, and he is my Protector, my Savior. I am fearless and brave when I know He is always watching over me. I do not feel I am alone; I have the great Power to guide me and support me. I know He has life under control, and everything He does,

He does for a reason, and I will not resist Him nor the pleasures life brings. When I keep my faith in Jehovah strong and sturdy, my steps remain strong and steady in turn.

It is also important to have faith in someone. You need a supporter through hard times, a friend you can count on with your life, someone you can confide in without any hesitation. I know how difficult it can be to find a person you can trust with your life. If you cannot find someone like that, at least have a person you will trust enough with secrets and your deepest feelings. I am a lucky one, for I have a person in whom I have faith like a newborn. The special person in my life is my beloved mother Juliet Cheng, who, besides God, is the cornerstone and the light of my life, and the foundation of my happiness, strength, and success. She is my best friend, my cheerleader, my advisor, and my sidekick, all in one wonderful being.

Faith in God has played a huge role in both my mother's and my lives. She held her deep faith as she battled both of her custody cases with doctors in America in order to save my life. And I held deep faith in her as she fought, for I knew she would win. Later in life, I began having faith in God, and it gives me strength to move forward. So I have a Heavenly Father and an earthly mother to love and watch over me. I will be forever grateful to God for giving me such a wonderful mother.

Gratitude

Although it may sound easy, many, many people cannot achieve total and complete gratitude. Sure, you may be grateful when the sun is shining, the sky is blue. But what if black clouds roll in and the sky decides to cry? Would you still be grateful? Would you be grateful that you had the privilege to experience the sunshine and blue sky in the past?

The most important and useful gratitude you can ever possess is the gratitude for both your sunny days and your dark days. If you can truly be grateful while at your lowest, primitive level—while you have only yourself left in life—you will be able to face any difficulties.

Appreciate today and its riches. Be thankful for the gems that sparkle; focus on the gifts God has bestowed upon you. Do not let any dust or dirt tarnish the value of these diamonds; the dirt itself cannot touch or harm the treasures—only you have the power to ultimately soil the gems, so handle them with grace and appreciation. For each day that passes, thank God for that day and its riches. Instead of waiting for disaster to strike in order to be thankful for what little is left after its devastation, love and appreciate everything and everyone right now.

Start everything with appreciation. Before you start anything new, say anything new, go anywhere new, first appreciate your current state in every aspect. This appreciation will act like a cushion if you ever fall back to where you started, your original state. So if you are thankful for now, when you return to now, you will continue to be thankful. Once you have achieved gratitude from the beginning, you will not fear losses; you will be thankful for everything you will gain, even in the tiniest amount.

Appreciate challenges and setbacks. Be grateful for the challenges that have given you setbacks. Learn from what went wrong to avoid it the next time.

Have a moment to reflect on life and your past. What parts of life have taught you lessons, have made you wiser, have made your spirit stronger? Are they not challenges? Challenges are exercising machines for your mind and spirit. Life gives us many treasures to be thankful for, and the gifts that make you stronger are challenges. I believe challenges are life's vaccines. They equip your soul with the necessary tools to battle future storms. I have received many of these vaccines; the challenges and obstacles have left numerous scars on my body in all shapes and sizes, but these marks have made me stronger and more invincible as I wait for the next high mountain to scale. I relish the taste of victory each and every time I battle and win. If there were no challenges, how could I name myself a victor? If there were no darkness, how could the stars appear so bright?

But many people do not realize the value of challenges. Instead, they see them as roadblocks, and feel frustrated when they encounter a challenge or an obstacle. They then feel trapped and stuck. They feel they have no where to go, but that is not true. Whenever a door is closed to me, I find another door to open. There are plenty of other avenues to explore. What may seem like a block may actually lead you in a better direction, with more opportunities than the road you were previously traveling.

When you climb five steps on your ladder and fall back two steps, you still achieved three steps, so be grateful for those three steps of progress.

Although I have lost my eyesight and the ability to walk, I do not scorn life; I am not mad at God for taking away my power to see and the gift of full mobility; instead, I am grateful for having owned these gifts before. I am content with what I have, so I use my time on Earth to enjoy life to the fullest. Why should I worsen my life by being miserable?

I am extremely grateful to God for giving me my life. I am grateful for each and every day. I am honored and privileged to be able to experience living. I am honored that He has chosen me to live, so I want to express my sincerest heartfelt gratitude and show him how much I love my life. I know that there is always someone out there who is in a worse situation than I am in, so I am thankful for what and whom I have.

When you are given life, hold on to it

tightly yet delicately; cherish what has been given to you: your privilege to enjoy dawn's first rays, your power to give words of comfort to a stranger, and your fortune to receive warm embraces after a good cry. If you allow your mishaps to cloud these treasures—or do not realize the true value of challenges—you will make your situation worse than it is already, losing every good thing you do have. And watch out for the thieves who try to belittle your gifts; they are the people who refuse to recognize the worth of life.

So next time when you see a butterfly fluttering among wildflowers or hear a songbird's song, smile. You have the privilege to be in this life. There are millions of less unfortunate souls, and think of those infinite souls that have never been born to know this, to experience all this... I know I am one darn lucky gal!

Values

What are your values? What aspects in life do you feel are important? What qualities do you want to have and be associated with? When you identify your values, you will know what truly matters to you in life. Then you can successfully recognize your main goals in life. These are your fundamental goals, the goals that will affect the other goals you will make in life. For example, my personal value is goodness. I desire to be a good person, with good intentions. I want to bring good to others. So I base my goals on that value. I will then be satisfied with having achieved that value if nothing else.

Without values and beliefs, you will be lost. You will not have a sense of direction in life. Two plus two makes four. If you believe that two plus two makes everything and anything, you will undoubtedly encounter problems in your life. Your values are what you base your decisions on. You seek things in life using your values. Your values are your guide, your beacon. Once you have established firm values and beliefs, you will know exactly where you would want to go in life and which roads you will take to get there. You will have a good idea what your life's purpose is.

Your values and your beliefs create a lasting reality. Focus on them. Everything is impermanent in life—nothing you gain in material is ever guaranteed. Your house, your car, your job, your money, and even the people you love, can all be taken away from you. But no one and nothing can take away your values and principles if you do not allow them to. Your values and beliefs cannot be destroyed unless you destroy them yourself. Always prepare for material loss in life. As long as you maintain a strong spirit, you will be able to face your reality. You will not experience too much fear of loss if you give up the materials you have gained.

Love

Ah, the lovely, mysterious feeling. From love, all beautiful things bloom.

Loving Life

Loving life unconditionally goes hand in hand with gratitude—being grateful for your life unconditionally. Many people have asked me, "What inspires you?" I have always given my four-letter answer: life. The last time I gave this answer (during my third book signing at my local Borders Books & Music), the lady who works there laughed. She said that whereas I love life, people usually complain about life.

When things go wrong in people's lives, or when they do not get what they want, they start complaining about life. But does life ever complain about you? No matter how many times you have made a mistake, has the sun ever left your side? Have the birds ever stopped singing to you? Why do you not return that unconditional love?

Value life as is, in its purest form. Love the purity of life, which I do. What do I mean by the purity of life? Well, when you think about it, most problems in life, except for natural disasters and some diseases, are caused by humans. When you brush away those manmade problems, what is left is life in its purest form. And this is what I am in love with. Yes, call me a lovesick gal! But let me ask you this, what would you have missed if your existence had never existed? I know I am able to laugh; I am able to weep. Without my life, I would be able to do none of these.

To love and accept life is to love and accept God. When you love someone, what they do, what they say, even the places they visit and their own belongings, become more interesting and significant to you. Worshipping the ground they walk on would no longer seem so farfetched. To a parent, their child's drawing is much more precious than any famous masterpiece. To a lover's ears, the very name of the one they love is musical. You would more likely take the advice from someone you trust than that from a stranger. A simple gift from a friend is more valuable than an expensive present given by your least favorite person. I remember the pretty doll my mother gave to me for my fourth birthday when we were in China. I loved it dearly. It was so much more special because it was from my mother's heart. The gift, even if bedecked with real gold and silver, would not mean much to me if it was from someone else. So how you feel about someone will reflect in your feelings for what the person does, says, or gives.

Show your love for God by loving life. Love all His creations and the gifts to you. Be serious about life, for the value of life is immeasurable. But also have a grand time, for life is all about the bliss.

Loving Yourself

You may associate loving yourself with being selfish. It may be selfish, but selfish in a good way. Read on to see how.

You have to be your own true best friend in order to be the true best friend of the world. There are some simple dance steps you can take in order to accomplish it. I call them dance steps because becoming a true friend is all about dancing with your heart.

What do you see when people dance? Is it how their hands and feet move so gracefully in such unison with one another, yet each of them sparkles with individuality? Are the dancers smiling? What does that mean? They may be joyous when they move their bodies to the rhythm of the music, but that is not all. They smile because they are dancing with their hearts.

When you are dancing with your heart, you are dancing together with your heart and dancing using your heart, and as a result, you are becoming a dancing heart yourself.

What do you feel when you see people dance? Does that not get your emotions going? Does that not make you want to get up and dance, too?

When you dance, you project how you feel and what you feel onto any onlookers, causing them to have a desire, a need, to mirror your feelings and actions. You set good examples of life when you dance; you are teaching true things of life, so you must lead others by dancing yourself.

To dance with your heart, you must be pure. Release all the negative feelings hammering inside you and block out the ugly voices the outside world whispers stealthily in your ears. Just like a closet, you need to clean out all the junk and useless things in order to make room for good stuff or to find the treasures. Then take the following dance steps on your own before you can hold hands with your heart, and others can follow in your dance steps so they, too, can dance with their hearts.

- ❖ I mentioned your values—what you hold highest. Ask yourself, what qualities do you want in a friend? Do you want your friend to be loving, caring, honest, sincere, and trustworthy? Do you want someone you can trust and with whom you can share laughter and tears? Then those are the qualities you need to have in order to attract yourself. Others will be attracted to you, too.
- ❖ Accept who you are as a whole. Accept how you feel. Accept how you think. Accept how you look from your head to your toes. You may not like to accept yourself as you are now because you feel you are not perfect. But what is perfection anyway? Is nature perfect? If so, you must be perfect, too. Take a look—I bet that tall tree in your backyard

has at least one torn branch, but is it still majestic? Does it still deserve to be called beautiful? Perfect? Acknowledge your flaws, focus on what good things you do have, and expand on those good qualities. When you accept your life, your position, your purpose, you will likely accept the lives, positions, and purposes of others.

- ❖ Be open, truthful, and honest with yourself. Do not lie to yourself. Do not live with pretense. When something is making you unhappy, face it, do not run away from it. Change the situation with a clear and honest look. By closely examining the situation you are in, you will be able to find the root of the problem and plug it out. By remaining in the dark, you will never find that root, so turn on the lights! Being honest does not simply mean not telling lies. Actions speak louder than words. If your actions are dishonest, you are not an honest person. If you shoplifted at your local store and then donated some money to your local church, would you be honest? If you go to church on Sundays and cheat on your spouse on Tuesdays, would you be honest?
- ❖ Understand your feelings, thoughts, and why you behave the way you do. Find the purpose to your actions. Learn from your past and those situations that did

not go as smoothly as hoped, and utilize what you learn to make your future bright.
- ❖ Honestly tell yourself, "I know I am not a bad person. I know I do my best in everything I do, and I know I am being my best, so I love myself because I am a good person with good intentions."
- ❖ Appreciate what and whom you have. Appreciate what you are able to do. If you cannot appreciate yourself, how can you appreciate other people, especially when their situation is in a lower state than yours? For example, some people cannot understand why the heck I am so happy. How could I possibly be happy when I cannot see and walk? They do not understand because they, themselves, do not appreciate their own lives even though they can both see and walk.
- ❖ Count your blessings. Focus on the good things you do have at the present and the positive side of things. Do not dwell on bad situations, but instead, move forward and have a bright attitude and outlook for the future. You have the ability to make a difference to your future just by being positive. Choosing the road to positivity and happiness will give you the strength, the desire, and the motivation to take giant steps forward. Do not pick the road to misery—it will just glue you to one spot, and you would

not want to get the glue onto others, now would you?

- ❖ Be passionate about who you are and what you do. Value life; cherish every minute that is given to you. Hold on tightly to the happy moments and their memories because when they are gone, they are gone forever. Live with conviction; live with vitality.
- ❖ Smile often. Smile to yourself, even if there is no good reason. Smiling will warm you up, even when the days seem dreary. Frequently treat yourself to a big smile while working or frolicking; it is the sweetest treat you can give yourself, and the best part is that there are no calories!
- ❖ Lastly, think about two kinds of friends: those who choose whom to be nice to, and those who are nice to everyone. You know, the Sarah who is nice to only the popular girls and mean to the girl next door. Is that person with whom you want to be friends? And there is Mary who is nice to everyone she knows and meets—what do you think of her? Does she sound as though she would make a good friend? So which person's trait would you like to possess yourself?

Achieving these dance steps, of course, by no means will make everyone like you, but this will make you feel better about yourself and the world. I know all this because—you guessed it—I am a dancing heart!

Above all, to love yourself definitely does not mean that you should be a selfish, arrogant person. It is all about appreciating your life and the lives of others. If you love yourself only, all the love you can ever receive in return is your own; no one else's. But you will have to start with yourself and end with others to make the circle complete.

You ultimately live for others, not yourself. Living solely for yourself will create an empty life, with not much purpose. Think about it—this universe is in existence not only for you, it exists for everyone. And it needs all the love it can get from everyone! We ultimately live for one another's happiness, craving one another's love. So yes, you love yourself to be happy—happy because you are appreciated and loved back. That does have a selfish streak to it, but it is a good one at that, is it not?

Loving Others

Take my love, and do as you wish with it. I expect nothing in return, no acknowledgement, no obligation; for loving you is the biggest reward itself; it gives me complete happiness.

Love is humble, love is meek; it should not be boastful nor proud. Love knows no time, love knows no distance; love shortens the distance between you and the one you love. Love is like the wind: as gentle as a summer's breeze and as strong as the stormy winds; you can not see it, but you can easily feel it. When you can love in secrecy, you will have achieved true love. When you can love without fearing any loss, without feeling that you have sacrificed in any way, you have found true love within. There is no need for others to know of your love, to pry into your heart, so do not brag or boast of your love.

When you love someone, do not expect love to be returned. Be patient, be hopeful, but do not expect. Love is an element that comes naturally, unplanned and unexpected. It cannot be forced or rushed. Love someone for who they are from the inside to the outside. Love acknowledges flaws and faults and is not critical. If you want to change someone, you would not be loving that person; you would be loving someone new and different, unless he or she wants to change on his or her own.

Since love comes naturally and cannot be forced, not everyone can love anyone. It is hard to love those who are unlovable. But even if you do not love someone for any reason, still treat them with respect, like a human being. I would rather be wronged than do wrong myself. The same goes for being respectful: if someone treats me wrongly, I should keep my head high and not strike back with disrespect. If I do not love someone, I should not hate them, either.

Love others equally. Treat paupers the way you would treat kings. Show no less kindness and respect toward the sickly, the poor, and the elderly than toward the wealthy, the handsome, and the healthy.

It tends to be easy to maintain relationships, from friendships to marriages, when the days are bright. True love is tested when people face mountains in life. We laugh together, but can we always endure together? Marriages break apart when a partner gets ill, grows old and gray, or becomes less attractive, causing the other partner to abandon their marriage vows. If you can endure hardships, hand in hand, you know you have true love. True love is brightest when days are darkest.

Hope

The last component in your foundation is a tender, gentle, but powerful element. Hope is like the cherry on top of an ice-cream sundae. Without it, the dessert will not seem so perfect, yet it is a small part of the sundae. Many times, I save the cherry for last, so I will have something to look forward to. Hope is the first spark of flame that turns into a bonfire. It gently nudges you forward in life. It demands nothing but gives abundantly.

Faith is having conviction that things will go right, whereas hope is wishing that things will go right. If you cannot have faith in something, at least have hope. Hope is like a seed that can sprout, grow, and bring forth fruits, as long as you nourish and maintain the seed within.

The best kind of hope is hope in God, as with any other element in life.

After this chapter, you will read my personal story of hope, and how it has positively impacted both my mother's and my lives.

So these are the five principles that make up the foundation. Once you have established unconditional faith, gratitude, love, and hope, and determined your values, you will be able to build on that foundation to make your life truly successful. Even if others pluck fruits off your tree and eat them all up, you will be able to bear fruits over and over again, as long as your foundation is firmly planted. And even if you lose everything you have built, you will still have the foundation from which to build again. You have done it the first time, so you can do it again and again and again.

What feeds the tree, you ask? Food and nutrients. Humans need the basic life's necessities—food and water—in order to survive, but that is to exist only. In order to live, to live with purpose and passion, you need the spiritual foundation.

Always a Tomorrow

Nature is filled with hope. You will find hope in every crevice and corner of the world: from the sprouting seed that hopes for rain to help it grow strong and tall, to the hatchling that hopes for food as it keeps its beak wide open, waiting for its mother to feed it a juicy insect to gobble down. A woman will hope for the best with every pregnancy, whereas a man will hope for strong hands to earn a living for his family.

Hope plays a vital role in life. Its arms gently wrap around the hopeful one to wish for the best, without truly demanding the best. It asks for nothing but gives abundantly.

It is with deep hope how both my beloved mother Juliet Cheng and I have endured our trials and tribulations and conquered all the challenges and obstacles, with grace. When she became pregnant, God planted the seed of hope deep in her heart so she could face what lay ahead. Plenty of hardship has certainly lurked in the shadows of our lives, yet we know there will always be a tomorrow.

Our long, rugged journey began with the tuberculin skin test I received before my first birthday. In five days, I had a fever of 104 degrees, and to my mother's horror and shock, it quickly developed into severe juvenile rheumatoid arthritis. My major joints became red, swollen, and agonizingly painful, making everyday chores, like dressing and bathing, highly difficult. Nights were spent with my mother rocking me to sleep, often long into the early morning. She became physically worn down and exhausted. Twenty-four hours and seven days a week were used up for me. Yet, she accepted our fate and endured the hardship with no word of complaint. She gritted her teeth and tenaciously moved on. She knew she would strongly stand by my side and that she would never give up for my sake. She promised to make life the best experience for me. Deep down inside, she knew we were watched over by God. It was His plan, as unfathomable as it was, so it was futile to be angry, have vengeance upon her heart, and question God about our lives. She knew whatever He did was for a reason, so she put all her hope and dreams in His hands.

Within a period of ten years, my mother brought me to China, her native country, six times, because American medications offered no relief for me; American doctors gave me aspirin, which only worsened my conditions and caused severe side effects. She saved my life by doing so, for I had knocked on death's door several times. Every time the plane took off for China, her hope soared higher than the plane.

Once in China, at age four, I was actually able to walk while receiving effective shots combined with massage therapy. For the first time, she had really tasted the sweetness of the fruit of hope; and for me, I explored a world I had never really known: the world outside of hospital walls. I was fascinated by everything I saw, heard, and touched, experiencing the new feelings that come with walking, running, and dancing. I caught bugs of all shapes and sizes, ranging from black spiders to bumble bees—none scared me—and studied them intensively. I tasted the freedom of discovery that I never knew existed. I felt alive as I chased after butterflies and picked wildflowers alongside the hospital where I was admitted.

Sadly, my walking days ended a year later when the quality of the shots went downhill, but my high spirit and hope (my mother had given me a huge chunk of her hope, as hope is contagious) did not leave me. I continued to admire the outside world through my hospital or home windows, daydreaming of those good old days I would hopefully be able to relive again. And as for my mother—the hope in her did not wither and die; the seed had long sprouted, blossomed, and grew more so. With every passing day, she hoped for a new beginning, a next day, a bright tomorrow...

Our hope paid off when I was eleven: my health was finally stabilized, so for the very first time, I began schooling. I had been much too ill to learn in the prior years, so I was thrilled to be obtaining an education at last. Having been brought up in a single, Chinese-speaking family with no influence on education, I knew only my ABCs and very few simple English words. I knew that two plus two equals four and that three times five is fifteen. I had no idea from where rain comes or why we see a rainbow after a refreshing rain. How I yearned to read a book or write down what my heart longed to say! Every time I saw a yellow school bus pass by, I wished I were one of the students lucky enough to ride in it. It puzzled — and still puzzles — me why there are more frowns than smiles on many faces of students. There is so much that needs to be learned, probed, and discovered. How could I live without understanding the Earth where I call home? How could I not want to learn more about the elements that make up who I am?

I started schooling in a special education class in elementary school. I was highly excited about going to school for the very first time, and on the first day, I rose from my bed with high spirits. I was hopeful that I would enjoy going to school and learning. I was hopeful that my teacher would be kind and patient, and that my classmates would become my good friends. Above all, I was hopeful that I could catch up to those students who had already had five years of schooling.

My first day of school glided by smoothly, and I instantly befriended my teacher (who, I was pleasantly surprised, was very kind) and classmates, holding high gratitude in my heart for the teacher who would bring me one of the most precious gifts in life.

After returning home that day, I began my journey into reading with the simple picture book picked out by my teacher. I could not read a single sentence, so my mother went over each word with me. Within an hour or two, I was able to read nearly the entire book by myself with perfect pronunciation. I practiced reading the book for a few days until I made certain I could read every word with ease. Every day thereafter, I brought home a new book to read. Within the first few weeks of school, I had filled two notebooks with poetry, and shortly thereafter, I was reading at fourth-grade level. I was floating on Cloud Nine; no longer was I lying on my hospital bed daydreaming about school and reading—my dream had finally come true.

After about 180 days of attendance (during which I went to China for the sixth and last time), my special education teacher told my mother: "She's ready to go to a regular sixth grade class, and she'll do very well in it," for I had mastered grade level in all areas.

Thus, I eagerly swam into the mainstream system, fishing numerous awards (including Student of the Year in sixth grade, Student of the Month in seventh grade, and an excellence award for achieving the highest grade of ninety-seven in Earth science in the entire eighth grade class) along the way. I entered high school with a smile that spoke a thousand words.

Every obstacle, every barrier, I have run into, has miserably failed to injure my spirit and dampen my hope, not even the latest turning-point stone life threw at me when I was seventeen: the loss of my eyesight. Being an artist of the visual arts, it is a great loss for me; I miss immensely seeing the beauty of our world, although all that I have known and seen are tucked safely in my memory book, deep in my heart. I continue to hope for the best and that I will someday behold the world again, but until that day comes, I do not stumble; instead, I dance gleefully, for my heart tells me all it sees as we glide far and wide.

My vision deteriorated during my sophomore year in high school. During that time, I learned only by listening to my teachers as they taught math, chemistry, and French, and yet, I still maintained A's.

My eyesight completely forsook me in April of tenth grade, so I had no choice but to stop attending school, and I received home-tutoring from the tutors my school sent. I completed all of my assignments strictly by using tape recorders, listening to the materials (e.g., homework, exams) and recording my answers and essays on cassette tapes from which my teachers graded me. I also successfully balanced and wrote long chemistry equations in my head without vision or Braille (I cannot use Braille because of my severe arthritis).

As much as I wanted to earn a diploma from my high school, I could not—I accumulated only half of the credits required to graduate (from these credits, however, I earned an overall average of ninety-seven, which is a GPA of 3.9, without any advanced placement classes)—so I earned my high school equivalency diploma instead. I took the GED exam, including mathematical calculations and problem solving, graphs, and an essay, without the aid of vision, and yet, I earned a special recognition award for receiving an exceptionally high score of 3280. I was a student speaker at my graduation ceremony, and was the only one who received a thunderous standing ovation after speaking.

Since I no longer could depict life's many fascinations through artwork, I turned to writing to express my thoughts and emotions, and to share with others my imagined worlds and creations. I began my career as a writer when I was twenty, and by the time I knew it, I had written three books within one year.

I am so thankful to live in times of technological advances, for a screen reader (computer software) has enabled me to become a writer when it would otherwise have been impossible. The reader tells me which keys I type and reads the text on the screen, except graphic text. Because of my arthritis, I can type with only my two index fingers, but I manage it quite well, typing at the speed of about sixty words per minute. Not only have I written the books entirely on my own, but I have also successfully completed every self-publishing task, including formatting my manuscripts, by myself. I also design and maintain my own website. That is what plenty of hope does to a blind individual!

Every time I think about the past, it brings a smile to my face, even when I recollect the dark days, for my mother's hope and mine has sought out the light amid every dark tunnel.

I see the long, rugged road stretching seemingly endlessly ahead of us, but I am unafraid to follow it and persist onward. Instead, my soul excitedly tingles with hope for every minute of the future. I have much more to achieve, to experience, to know; I have much to give, to show, to express; and only with a hopeful heart can I achieve all that I yearn to achieve.

No mountain is high enough to hold me back; no wind is strong enough to blow me down. There are stars I must reach; there are roads I must take, and with my blooming hope inside, I spread my wings wide to embrace all that tomorrow will bring.

Are You Happy?

Are you happy? Are you truly, seriously, undoubtedly happy right this minute? Well, your answer may be yes since you probably had something good happen to you. But let us pretend that nothing "extraordinary" has happened. Would you still be happy? Are you happy with your life, with yourself? Sure, your life is not perfect (no one's is) but how many things in your life are you happy and content about? (Wait, do not answer that yet—you might give me "Not much!")

No person or thing can make you truly happy—only you have the power to create happiness in your life. God can truly make you happy, but if you do not accept Him, how could He bring you happiness? You may be as wealthy as Bill Gates and have all the friends in the world, but if you do not like and appreciate yourself for any reason, you will not feel happy.

You first have to allow happiness into your life. You have to accept the happiness the world gives you by appreciating what life offers.

The first step in creating happiness in your life is to accept God's gifts. The biggest gift He has given to you is you. Therefore, you need to accept and be happy with yourself. Your opinion of yourself is the most important opinion of all. Others can say how great you are, but if you think otherwise, it will not bring you total and absolute happiness.

The key in being truly happy is knowing how to appreciate the "small" things in life. You will not be a very happy person if you expect huge materialistic rewards out of life or great benefits from others. Happiness is not about the quantity; it is about the quality. And by quality, I do not mean wealth. You need to appreciate the quality of the purity of life. Remember that the purity of life is everything minus the manmade problems. When you brush away those problems, you will then be able to see the purity of life.

Let us take my life as an example. I believe I was a very grateful child. True, I did not know about the concept of gratitude, along with other virtues of life, as I was merely an infant, but I was a very happy infant. Happiness starts with gratitude, especially the kind of happiness held by those who are in a less fortunate state than others. I was nicknamed the Happy Baby. Now you might think that I probably had a great childhood, filled with friends, toys, and good people. Although I do have the best mother, my life was filled with intense pain that cut through my joints like knives. Yet, I smiled through my tears, laughed between sobs, and my misty eyes lit up when I caught something pretty in the room. I still remember pointing at pretty dresses as I cried my little heart out. Surely, I was grateful just to exist?

I was happy, for I loved — and still love — life.

I must say that I am one of those few lucky people who have been born with a happy nature. But it is not too hard to acquire happiness even if you are not born this way. The thing to ask yourself is, "Do I want to be happy?" Answering yes will not do anything for you; you have to commit to that yes and to finding that happiness.

In life, there are always two roads from which to choose: the road to happiness and the road to misery. By picking the road to misery, you will put yourself in a more miserable situation than the one you are already in; plus, you will spread your misery on to others, making those around you miserable as well.

I am not telling you to jump for joy when someone close to you passes away or after you lose your job or have your heart broken. The thing to remember is that whatever happens to you, life moves on, and you need to decide whether you want to move on with it.

Who would not want to be happy? Although the answer may be obvious, it appears to me that very few are truly serious about living with happiness. People's focus is easily diverted when a negative comment comes their way or when something does not go as planned. Keep your eye on your goal of being happy, and then you will find it quite easy to remain happy.

If you are happy, you will enjoy what is

around you more; you will make others around you happy. You will make more friends, enjoy what you do and say, and cherish life more.

Happy people are more successful in life because they are able to move on and achieve; they do not dwell on the negativity that surrounds them. Instead, they are thankful for every progress they make and even the challenges they face. I know this, for I am not known as the Happy Princess for nothing.

So how many things in your life are you happy and content about?

Branches of Spiritual Success

Now that we have discussed the foundation with the five essential elements — faith, gratitude, values, love, and hope — I would like to cover the major branches that spring from those ingredients.

Courage is a main branch from faith, and the courage you receive after embracing God is the most rewarding courage there is. When you have faith in God, you will have courage to face life's challenges, as you will know He is there watching over you. The faith in God will give you strength to take your giant steps forward. Courage is a great virtue, but it is born from faith. When you have faith in someone, you will be able to trust that person during tough situations, and in turn, you will have courage to fight, without feeling that you are alone to deal with difficulties. You will also have courage when you have unwavering faith in yourself. When you do not fear losses, nothing can stop you.

Happiness is a major branch that comes from both gratitude and love. You find happiness in the things and people you are grateful for and love. Without loving yourself, how could you be happy about yourself? Without loving others, how could you be happy around them? If you cannot be grateful for something, how can you be happy about it? If you cannot be grateful for your existence while you are at your lowest state, how can you be happy about your situation? When you are grateful for the smallest things, you will feel happy and content for what you have and will not fret over the things you do not have.

Forgiveness comes from love. When we are sorry for something we did wrong, we hope that others could forgive us. So why could we not forgive others when they are sorry for what they did wrong? But even if they are not sorry for their wrongdoing, why make ourselves suffer more? We have already endured their wrongdoing, and that is enough. To resent what they did will hurt us more, so it is vital to move on. Why let them harm us more by holding anger in our hearts? Do not fall into the trap of wrongdoers, for many wrongdoers enjoy seeing us upset when they did us wrong. Let them fail in their attempt to make us upset and hold a grudge.

People say forgive and forget, but true forgiveness means that you can recall the situation without any negative feelings. Of course, if we forget something, we would automatically forgive it. So true forgiveness is when you *are* able to remember what happened to you without any negative feelings. If you no longer feel angry or upset, you have achieved forgiveness. It is important to forgive in order to move forward. Without forgiveness, you would be dwelling in your past. Does holding a grudge do you any good? Would it make you feel better? Would it change what happened to you? No, it would not; instead, it will just make things worse. Putting what happened behind you will help you feel better and will allow you to give your full attention and focus to what is truly important to you.

I am one who simply remembers things—the good, the bad, and the ugly. The past is a part of my life. Why should I forget what I have experienced, felt, and learned? But I am forgiving; I do not recall what happened to me with hatred or bitterness. I sometimes just shake my head at a bad memory and think, "There are all kinds that make up this world," and move on.

Do not seek revenge for other people's wrongdoing. If someone did you wrong, do not do that person wrong in return. Let wrongdoing be done by wrongdoers only.

Passion stems from both values and love. It is easy to understand why passion can come from love—you will automatically be passionate about what you love to do and whom you love.

But how does passion come from your values?

Passion is the reason why you love to do something. When you ask why, your answer would be your value. For example, you may be passionate about teaching because you love being a teacher. Why are you passionate about teaching? Sure, you may like to be with kids, but there is a deeper reason, and that reason is your belief that children should be well educated at an early age by a good teacher. So that is your value. Why do I love to write? The reason I am passionate about writing is that I am able to inspire others, to bring a bit of good to other people's lives. I believe that good books can positively affect a person's life.

Patience, tolerance, respect, understanding, and honor come from a loving person (did I not say all wonderful elements bloom from love?). You do not need to love a person in order to respect them or to understand their needs, as long as you have a loving heart.

For instance, love (with all its branches) and common sense (life smarts that come naturally) are the ingredients that make any person knowledgeable about the needs of the sickly and the frail. If you lack these two most important elements—even if you have all the knowledge in the world—you will not be a good caregiver at all. That is why I have faced so many problems with doctors and officials. They may be experts in their fields, but they do not know anything about my needs when they lack love and common sense. My mother has both love and common sense in full abundance, so she is the smartest doctor I have ever met.

Love and common sense are the best elements you can bring with you to your workplace, to your school, or in everyday living, for that matter. Always have an open heart and ears to listen to the voices of others in need. You may not fully understand their needs or problems, but respect them. Do your best in accommodating their needs and requirements. Do not just use your brain, use your heart more often. By doing so, you are setting good examples for others, including your fellow professionals. See that others are happy, not just healthier, richer, or more successful. Life is all about happiness, being there for one another, and being life smart.

A loving person will be able to respect and honor others even if the relationship lacks love. For example, you need to honor your parents even if they did you wrong. After all, God has chosen them to bring you into this world. You may not like who they are, but they are the only people who created you. Without them, you would not exist. You would not be here with the ability to enjoy life. So you will have to thank your parents for giving you this great opportunity.

In the following pages, I would like to share with you the moment when my mother and I first met: my own birth, a precious moment both my mother and I hold dear to our hearts.

I describe my mother with one sentence: "She's a fighter, a victor, but above all, she's a lover." She embraces all that surrounds her despite the harshness of the world. Not only has she stood up for me countless times, she has also saved my life numerous times from the grasp of death. I am very serious when I say that if it had not been for her, I would not be here today.

She is what I call an ultra-abled mother, and you will know why when you read the following story. Not only has she given me such a wonderful life filled with unconditional love, but she had started my life in the most beautiful way...

I am darn proud to have her as my mother.

The Brave Bringer of Life

The strong wind whirled, bringing dancing flakes in its invisible arms, equally distributing a thin layer of snow to other places of the frozen land. Small spheres of shimmering, crystalline flowers alighted upon the earth from their silvery home above, while the sun still slept peacefully below the horizon during this misty dawn. The sky jewels still twinkled ardently, as if calling news of most importance. Although the air was still and cold, it did not lack any emptiness. Faint songs of birds accented one another in counter harmony. Many creatures had packed their bags and sought shelter elsewhere, in a land of abundant warmth and merriment; some others snuggled cozily in their lairs for their long sleep.

And it was on this January morning that our story takes place, of a gentle woman, who although in great physical pain, was filled with happiness of the most delicate nature. She was to contribute to the circle of life, secluded inside thick medical walls, where a new era in her life would take place...

"Push, push." The voices urged her onward, but all she could hear was the beating of her own heart. She wondered how could one heart beat so loudly. Was it because it was two hearts—a tiny life inside her and her own—beating as one? She lay on the bed, the sheets damp with the sweat that streamed down from her every pore. Her Oriental hair matted on her forehead. A new life would add to Earth's circle of life. That thought unconsciously swam in her mind, giving her the strength to do what the nurses had instructed: to push, push.

Her dark eyes focused on the ceiling above her as each contraction tore at her soul. Although it felt like a sharp knife was plunging deep into her, not a single cry of pain escaped her lips, nor did her eyes shed any tears. Instead, her heart danced with an immeasurable sense of exquisite joy. This was the most important day of her life, a day that would bring her forever happiness, so she gratefully took the bitterness to welcome the everlasting sweetness that was to follow. She and her child would spend the brightest and darkest days together, sharing all the surprises, both good and bad, that life would bestow upon them.

It was her first child, a gift given by the Heavenly Father, and she would use her whole heart and soul to treasure the jewel. Awe and love filled every crevice of her soul once she learned of her pregnancy, and for the past nine months, she had been wondering what the baby would be like. Would dimples decorate its cheeks when it smiled? Would it laugh when she clicked her tongue? She did not know whether it was a girl or boy. She had gone to do the ultrasound, but it had been too early to detect the sex of the baby. It would simply have to be a surprise, a wonderful surprise.

So, on she pushed against the paralyzing pain. Sweat continued to pour out, adding to the small river that was collecting on the sheets underneath her. Her surrounding was a complete blur to her as her only focus was bringing out a new life. Yet what the doctor said next sharply cut through her concentration.

"The baby has to come soon, or we will have to perform a caesarean section,"

The doctor's gentle, but urgent words seemed to be amplified against her hammering body.

All her energy was nearly drained, but the words charged her with new energy she never knew she could possess. Could she get her baby out in time, in time so—? She dared not finish that thought—she had no time to think. Her future—no, their future—now solely depended on her. Would she let both of them down? No, never. And after this victory of hers, she would climb to the highest peak and shout to the world she was a new mother.

Long seconds ticked by.

Time seemed to stand still. Seconds stretched on as minutes.

There was no time left. Not enough time left. She had no time to panic.

"Push, push," the chorus continued. Did they think that she would actually stop pushing if they ended the chant?

Then it happened, soundlessly.

No cry was audible, so one would have wondered if anything had indeed occurred if it had not been for the next words, which seemed to have come from afar. They sounded musical to the expecting woman's ears.

"A beautiful girl!" the doctor announced with a big smile.

That smile was not even close in matching the one on the new mother's face. She had made it. Yes, she was now an honest-to-goodness mother, no more labels such as the expectant mother that she was impatient to alter. A girl! How her heart fluttered in her chest. She had thought it would be a boy, and had the name "Jordan" ready. The baby was twelve days late, so a boy was thought to be the reason. Well, she was pleasantly wrong. She knew she could dress her little girl up in the prettiest of dresses, with ribbons and laces...

The nurse by the new mother's bedside smiled and gently patted her shoulder. "You are so brave; you did not cry even once!" She returned the woman's smile with a smile that spoke a thousand words.

The doctor brought the baby over to the new mother. The sight that met her eyes almost made her swoon with sheer delight, and vanquished any concerns she ever held. If the dictionary ever needed a definition for the perfect baby, she would describe her newborn. She was the most beautiful baby she had ever seen. She could not take her eyes off the child, from her head full of black hair down to her tiny feet. Her skin was as white and soft as the loveliest lily petals; not a single wrinkle was present, or any places of pinkness visible. In turn, the baby was returning the gaze with her large brown, penetrating eyes that were wide open, searching within her mother's soul.

We, at last, had found each other, twenty-four years ago. Each and every time I think about how lovingly my mother Juliet Cheng had brought me into this world — with no tears, only cries of joy, how could it not bring warmth to my heart? She ignored the pain of childbirth, and instead focused on the forthcoming fruit of her labor. And this is how she has raised me, by brushing away all the mountains with a kiss, promising sunshine for tomorrow. Thus, I celebrate her daily as she celebrated my birth. She bravely welcomed me into existence as we both entered a brave new world to journey, hand in hand.

Love the Life You Live

How can we fully enjoy what all life has to offer and succeed in life without torturing ourselves in the process? We are put on Earth to love life, nothing else. Yet, many times, we get so caught up in our everyday obstacles and manmade problems that we lose focus on our purpose and how to enjoy life. So we instead become our own slaves to the problems we have created ourselves.

Below are some things to do or keep in mind to help you focus on loving the life you live. They have all been born from personal experiences and nocturnal daydreaming and deep thinking.

Believe in God Almighty First and foremost, truly and honestly believe in God. A multitude of people claim they believe in God, but their actions do not match their words. How could they believe in God when they continually look down upon and take advantage of the poor, the sickly, and the elderly; engage in dishonest business practices; backstab their friends; give false testimonies under oath; shoplift and steal from other people's homes; and cheat? Would not the fear of God prevent them from doing wrong in the first place?

Just because you cannot see God does not

mean He cannot see you. He knows your every action, your every thought; He knows what you plan to do even before you do it. God tells us to fear Him, and I tell you to love Him with all your heart, with all your soul, and with all your strength, just as His beloved Son Jesus Christ commands. Show your love and belief in Jehovah by doing what is good. If you love someone, you would want to do what pleases that person. Do not love God because He promises everlasting life. Love God because He is your Heavenly Father. Would you love someone just because he or she promises you riches?

Denying God is like denying your human parents. Is the existence of everything not enough proof?

Find your purpose It is important to determine the purpose of your life. Otherwise, you will not live in a way that you would feel is fulfilling enough. A purpose can give you a sense of direction. Without a purpose, it will be the same as driving aimlessly without any destination in mind, unless aimless driving is your purpose. What do you feel is the purpose of life? Your life? People's opinions on the purpose of life can differ greatly. It does not matter if your purpose does not match anyone else's. As long as you have set your own purpose in life, you will then feel more fulfilled with life, especially when you arrive at your final destination.

Here is what I believe life is all about:

The purpose of life is to
1. Believe in Jehovah God
2. Enjoy life to the fullest extent possible
3. Positively contribute to at least one person's life
4. Be a good person
5. Do what is important to you
6. Establish and hold on to your values and beliefs
7. Thank God and count your blessings

Realize your importance You are the center of your life. You are the subject of your life. Without you, your life will not exist. All that you experience, all that you do, is unique to you. True, everything exists for everyone, but if you have never been born, what will the blazing sun matter to you when you are not here to experience it?

Put your needs first Take care of your needs first. It does not mean that you will turn into a selfish person. When you take care of yourself first, you will have the ability to continually care for others. If you constantly put the needs of others first and yours last, you will eventually use up all your energy and resources. And guess what happens? You will no longer be able to care for others, or yourself.

Mothers tend to be the group in nature that put the needs of others—of their children—first. My own mother is a good example of putting the needs of others first in line. She always cares for me and others first before caring for herself. As a result, I brokenheartedly see her energy and strength wasting away. I try to remind her that her own needs are very important, too, and that she should watch over her own health and needs first.

I had also seen the actions of a very selfless mother in a wildcat I used to study. Where we used to live, we had many wildcats at our backyard. They came onto our deck daily, and I enjoyed studying each and every one of them, as each had his or her unique personality. I can clearly recall a mother cat. She was very thin. She had a new litter of kittens, and she often stole food from our deck to feed them. I noticed that every time, she would feed them first and share the majority of the food, hesitatingly taking only the last bit of scraps. Very soon afterward, I did not see her anymore. Her kittens were left unattended. I believe that she had met her sad end, leaving behind kittens who still needed her care. In the end, only one kitten survived, as far as I know.

Be yourself Be who you are, as long as you know that you are a good person. Do not be forced to be who you are not, and do not be forced to do things that strongly go against your wishes and personal values, as long as you know that those wishes and values are not wrong. Many teenagers go through peer pressure when their friends and schoolmates dare them to do drugs and smoke with them, and many give in to the pressure to fit in. These teenagers become the people others order them to be, not the people they truly are. It is as though they have lost their own identity.

It is vital not to give in to other people's pressure and threats. You are the way you have been created, so you have the right to be who you are. If you truly believe in yourself, then be who you want. If you need guidance, seek guidance from those whom you trust and who are respectful in the society.

Also, do not pretend to be someone you are not. Many times, people do not feel others would like their real selves, so they act the way they feel would be more acceptable to others. Are other people's thoughts about you so much more important than losing your own identity and uniqueness?

You do not need to prove yourself to anyone. When you are nice to someone and you know it, do not do something extra to prove you are nice to that person. Let your words and actions be natural. If people do not appreciate your sincerity, that is their loss.

Learn how to say no You sometimes may not feel comfortable saying no for a number of reasons:

a) You are concerned that you may hurt other people's feelings or that you would upset them. Although receiving a no may be disappointing, it will not upset the person, unless they are not very understanding to start with. Why use up your energy on a person who is not understanding? It is their problem, not yours.

b) You think that you will delay other

people's work. If it is not life threatening or truly important, it will not matter too much to them. They can turn to others for help; you are most likely not the only resource they have. They can move on without you.

c) That it will make a huge difference to others. Many times, saying yes will not necessarily benefit them in their situation, so saying no will not negatively affect their situation, either.

Avoid blaming yourself unreasonably Do not criticize yourself. When you know you have done your best, when you have put your best effort in something, do not criticize yourself. Some people get upset or frustrated with themselves when they feel they did not do something perfectly. Keep in mind that perfection is simply an opinion, not a fact. Perfection is how you see something in a certain way, so everyone has a different way of labeling what is perfect. How do you determine perfection? What is perfection anyway? And when will you determine that what you have done is done to perfection? What if you never realize perfection but continue until you use up your energy, without being satisfied?

Do not blame yourself for a misfortune or mishap that cannot be prevented. If you have asked someone to buy something, and on the road the person got into a car accident, it would not be your fault. How would you know that the tragedy would strike? True, it would not have happened if you had not sent that person on an errand at the wrong time, but that is simply fate. Realize that accidents can and do strike anyone, anytime, and that you cannot be held responsible for them.

But if you have been told—or you know yourself—that you have done something wrong, admit your wrongdoing, apologize, repent, and do not commit the same offense again.

Prioritize the important things in your life Focus on what is important to your overall life. We may get caught in urgent matters, such as deadlines, and abandon what is truly important. We should not live to work, live to eat—we should eat and work to live.

You and your family are most important. Your needs come first before anyone else's. Your health comes first before education.

Block out everything on your mind first, then prioritize the important things in life, and devote yourself to those priorities first, and to any truly urgent things you must do now; it is all about scheduling things right. If what you need to do seems overwhelming, break your tasks down into smaller tasks. If you need to clean your house, looking at all the things you need to do can be overwhelming. Make a list of the tasks you need to perform, and focus on one item at a time.

You need order in your life so as not to be in chaos, but do not attempt to control life. With an orderly life, you prioritize your importance but let life flow and go with the current; with a controlling life, you are trying to make everything work the way you want it to. You will be fighting life, and you will lose. Be life's friend, not an enemy.

Lend a helping hand After caring for your needs, you should take care of those who need your help the most. The keyword is your help—not their help, not my help, but *your* help. So you should help those who are closest to you—your family, your friends, or any strangers you just met who need immediate help.

When you are available in someone else's life to be helpful, put your kindness to work and lend a helping hand. Do not care for those you have never met over caring for your family. Some people enjoy volunteering in their community, but at home, they do little to help out. Some would rather donate generously to political parties, churches, and charities than save the money for the needy and the sickly right in their own homes. Many crave public recognition; good deeds done privately would not shine the spotlight on them (they forget all about God's attention, the most important of any attention). If you can help others behind closed doors, your help is true and honest.

Be completely helpful by finishing what you have intended or promised to do for others and do your best with it. Help is not so helpful if only half-complete.

If someone asks for bread, do not give

them fish. Sure, you can give fish with the bread (it is a good idea if you truly believe it is desirable), but not the fish alone. Give others what they ask for. Provide what they need. Something pretty but not useful will not be helpful. Treat others the way they want to be treated.

When you feel someone needs help, ask that person if he or she needs help. Not everyone is comfortable asking for help, so step in whenever you feel help is needed.

The most appreciated help is the kind where the recipient truly feels he or she had been helped, without feeling obligated to return the favor. Although we may ask for benefits in return in a strictly business setting, such as a joint venture or a win-win situation, expecting rewards after helping others in general is not the way to go. Do not make those you help feel like they owe you something, and in turn, they will feel like they owe you a ton of thanks! Ask only for the joy that comes with helping others in need. And when given straight from the heart, help brings smiles to both the giver and receiver. Now that is what I call a win-win situation!

Have fun and relax We are put on Earth to enjoy life and to experience all that life has to offer, good or bad. Do not always work, work, and work. Again, we are not here to live to work; we are here to work to live, but to have plenty of fun as well.

When you have achieved something,

celebrate. Learn how to stop working and relax for a while. Devote some time for yourself each and every day.

Many of us get a moment during the day when we feel the least productive and the most sluggish. If you have nothing important to do, use that period of time to relax. Do what you enjoy doing as a form of relaxation. For instance, I listen to music or read a good book when I want to relax. If nothing else, meditate.

Spend a moment to focus on you alone, as the primary energy in your life. When you block out everything, both the positive and the negative, in your surroundings, you are left with just yourself. It is as if you were left in an empty room, void of any sound, light, movement, smell, and taste. Then you will be completely in focus on your own self. This is when you can fully pay attention to yourself spiritually and physically, and when you can examine yourself as a spiritual being.

Relaxing brings you more energy. Your mind will be clearer for thinking and reasoning. You will be more focused on what you would want to achieve after you have determined your values and beliefs.

Without being relaxed — if you have all sorts of emotions bombarding you — you will not know what to focus on. It is as though you are an empty television channel, where it is loud and fuzzy, without containing any real or useful material.

If you have a million thoughts swimming

in your head at once, how could you focus on one thing? You need to focus on one thing at a time to complete things correctly—just as a doctor needs to focus on one patient at a time, and not think about his other patients while examining one patient.

Embrace modesty A humble heart is a good heart. A modest person is a wise person. If you open the door to arrogance, you will close the door to appreciation and acceptance of others or life in general. A humble soul can readily accept God into his or her heart and is grateful to Him. An arrogant spirit is a foolish one whose love for oneself is useless when that love does not attract love from others. The proud are also blind; they cannot see or admit their faults, so they will never learn; yet, they easily find or invent faults in others.

Do not look down upon others for any reason. Do not turn your heart away from the disabled; a car accident could send you to a wheelchair as well. Do not shun the not-so pretty; fire may scorch your face, too. Feed the poor as you are fed; warm the homeless as you are warmed.

Arrogance is fruitless. You may be smart, but there is always someone out there who is smarter; you may be handsome, but a handsomer person will always walk on Earth. But if you were pure, no one could humanly be purer. Purity is like white; no other color can be whiter. So aim for purity and start with humility.

Develop your spirituality Out of mind, body, and spirit, the spirit part of you is the most important. Your body acts like a vehicle for your mind and spirit.

If you have a strong spirit and a weak body, you will be able to overcome your limitations and rise well above others. On the other hand, if you have a strong body and a weak spirit, you will not be able to face life's challenges. Thus you need to build a spiritual foundation. Remember that tree! If you like, you can picture your favorite kind of fruit tree to help you remember your tree always. I love cherry blossoms, so a cherry blossom is the tree I picture. Although cherry blossoms do not produce fruits, the blossoms will be my desired end results — I want my achievements to be admired and appreciated by all, not gobbled up!

Admit your errors Admit that you are wrong when you are wrong. So many times, we want to save face and feel that it is the most important thing to save. But virtue is the best element to save. Is saving face so much more important than doing what is right?

If you have apologized for any wrong you have done, and people would not forgive you — do not worry. God is forgiving, and He will forgive you when you have admitted that you were wrong and promised that you will not commit the same error again. Why would people's opinions matter as long as Jehovah forgives you? What pleases Him most will be most important. The only opinion that counts is

His.

Expect no materialistic rewards or the spotlight Do not expect and crave for monetary rewards, material benefits, or public attention when you provide your resources. The greatest benefit should be the good feeling that comes from performing a kind deed; it surpasses all gold, silver, and jewels of the world. In general, do not crave materialistic benefits out of life or seek fame and notice from the human population; instead, seek approval from God.

When you do right in the eyes of Jehovah, He will reward you everlasting riches of the world. But do not do good just for His rewards; do good for the sake of goodness.

Forever will goodness prevail Remember, wrongdoers may win for a little while, but in the end, the victory will fall into the hands of those who are righteous.

The Power of Positivity

What is so important about positivity? What is the big deal anyway? Why do you need to be a positive person in order to achieve in life? To answer these questions, let us complete two simple exercises.

Exercise I

List seven positive things in your life, past or present. They can be anything: people, pets, places, activities, the abstract, and the intangible.

My personal list is:
1. God
2. My mother
3. Listening to oldies
4. Bird songs
5. Writing
6. Reading
7. Chocolate

What do all of your positive items have in common? Are they things you love? Do they make you happy?

In conclusion: Positive things, thoughts on positive things, make you happy. They can bring a smile to your face when you think about them.

Exercise II

Think of something you want to change in your life. It could be having a new career, starting a new relationship with someone you have had your eyes on for some time now, or trying out a new sport or activity.

Let us say you want to take a vacation in Europe. You have always wanted to tour the art museums and dine in the finest restaurants.

What does thinking about this positive change do for you?

In conclusion: Focusing on a positive goal, a positive thought, motivates you.

The Null of Negativity

Why is negativity such a distasteful element? What does it do to you? Let us find out by performing two simple exercises.

Exercise I

Write down seven negative things in your life, past or present.

My personal list contains:
1. Physical pain
2. The fright of nearly losing my mother twice during the custody cases
3. Having asthma attacks
4. Being mistreated by one-on-one aides when I attended school
5. Staying in hospitals
6. Losing my eyesight
7. Insomnia

Thinking about the negative items on your list, what feelings do you get?
In conclusion: Thoughts about negative things make you unhappy.

Exercise II

Go back to the second exercise we did for "The Power of Positivity." Instead of focusing on that dream vacation of yours and all the fun things you would do in Europe, think about all the obstacles and worries you would face. You might face language barriers, get lost, have your purse stolen by the clever pickpockets of Paris, or catch a bad case of travelers' diarrhea.

What does thinking about the negative aspects of your vacation do to you?

In conclusion: Thinking about the negative aspects of any situation can discourage you. It ruins your appetite and makes you less excited about your goal or situation. It makes you think twice about going after what you want.

When you are overwhelmed by a negative element in your life, think how you can turn it into a positive one. In most cases, every positive situation has a negative side, and every negative situation has a positive side. Sometimes, negative situations will actually turn out to be very positive.

Let us do an exercise together to find the positive side to a negativity. Look over your list of negative elements from the first exercise for "The Null of Negativity." Try to determine what positive elements they contain. You may have to think about the whole picture by examining every angle of the situation or issue.

The following list shows how I found the positive sides to my list of negative items.

1. *Physical pain*

Pain allows me to sympathize with those who experience physical pain. I believe that one has to taste the ordeal to truly understand what it is like and to have full sympathy for those who have experienced it. When you can see or hear and you say to a blind or deaf person, "Oh, I know how you feel," that would not be true. You could not really know how it feels without going through blindness or deafness yourself. Just because you fumbled around the room in darkness does not mean that you have experienced blindness.

2. *The fright of nearly losing my mother twice during the custody cases*

Because of the horror and injustice both my mother and I had experienced in the American medical system, I have become an advocate of parental rights in children's medical care to help today's loving parents protect and keep custody of their children, so they would not experience the horror we went through. When doctors ask yes or no, parents should have the right to say no.

3. *Having asthma attacks*

It strengthened my faith in God. When I was having an attack at age fourteen, I was running out of ways for relief; none of my emergency room visits could help. My mother then prayed to God with all her heart and soul, and instantly, the name of a medical center for emergency visits popped into her head. I received immediate relief from there.

4. *Being mistreated by one-on-one aides when I attended school*

I have become an advocate of aide/caregiver monitoring and screening for students with special needs and the disabled people in general.

5. *Staying in hospitals*

The hospital stays in China were quite beneficial, as my life was saved a few times, and I was able to walk for a full year at age four while receiving effective shots combined with massage therapy.

6. *Losing my eyesight*

After losing my sight, I became an author, motivational speaker, self-empowerment expert, and advocate! Need I say more?

7. *Insomnia*

Many great ideas for my writing come to me when I lie awake or sit in front of my laptop computer in the wee hours of the morning; most of this book was born this way.

Rise and Overcome!

Why do we have so much negativity, specifically the negativity that comes from people? It is because negativity comes in too many forms, easily outweighing the quiet and delicate positivity. Think about it for a minute: pure goodness can come in only one form, one order. I compare it to one specific order in a deck of cards. If you put the cards in order (positivity), and then you drop the deck, it will most likely go out of order (negativity). If you drop the cards five times, it will likely result in five different disorders (negativity). So as with a deck of cards, goodness has only one face while negativity has many faces. A good person will be good. A bad person may be a liar, a cheater, a thief, or a murderer; so bad apples come in all different forms. There is only one way to be good; there are countless ways to be bad. In essence, it is easier to be bad than it is to be good, therefore it is easier to be attracted to negativity than it is to be attracted to positivity. Since God does not control people's hearts, it is easy for many to move to the left a bit, to the right a bit, rather than keeping straight in life.

How do you ignore these many faces of negativity to live happily? The answer is in the question: you *must* ignore them to your best ability. If you truly, seriously, undoubtedly want a positive life, putting some effort in blocking out negativity will no longer seem hard; it will actually be invigorating. You must have the desire to live positively. You need one hundred percent desire for it; ninety-nine percent will not be enough to maintain it. If you are not finding and focusing on the positivity steadfastly, that tells me that your desires are not strong enough, no matter what you say. To read more about desires, flip to page 126.

It is vital to focus on positivity. Once you have established your desires for positivity, there are several things you can do or points to keep in mind to help you overcome negativity, remain positive, or at least, be thankful for your situation.

Life is full of obstacles and challenges; you would be fooling yourself to think otherwise. Before we run into any obstacle, we first need to prepare ourselves for negative or challenging situations. We need a cushion on which we can fall back when we run into life's hardships. Think about the acrobats performing in circuses: While they dazzle their audience with their skill and agility, nets below are ready to catch them if they ever fall. This is the kind of protection we need in life, so we will not become badly bruised once we crash down. This protection in life should be gratitude. Appreciation is the essential net to cushion us from ordeals, from everyday obstacles to life's traumas.

Start everything with appreciation.

Remember, before you do anything new, say anything new, go anywhere new, first appreciate your current state in every aspect. This acts like a cushion in the event that your actions return you to your original state. So it is vital to appreciate your situation at every stage of your life.

When you run into an obstacle, take the following steps to overcome it.

1. Calm down to focus on what you want to achieve. What can you do to deal with the situation? Focus on how to make your situation better. What might be the best actions to take in order to overcome your obstacle? You have to think outside your fear or negative emotions, so the first step to take is to calm down and put your feelings aside. Many times, your feelings amplify your problems. Negative emotions can put your values, beliefs, and desires in the background.

Worry, doubt, and fear stop rational thinking. Fear blocks and holds you back. It prevents you from examining your problem, stops your actions, and brings unbalanced emotions and spirit. If you remove fear, you will be able to examine the problem as is; then you can identify the area that is giving you difficulty.

When you live in fear, it feels as though time is flying past you, and that you have no more time left; you will feel suffocated, unable to move. It is like the physical reaction fear gives you. When you are in fear, your body tenses, not a muscle moves, and all of your body parts, including your hair, will go on the defense. Your mind either shuts down or there are too many thoughts going through your head, making it hard to think straight. That is what fear does to your spirit, too. Your body reflects how you are in spirit. If you are happy, you smile; if you are stunned, you lose colors.

2. Face the fact and fight. Let us say that you just got tossed overboard while cruising, would you not try your best to survive the mishap? What if you got stranded on a deserted island? You would not just stand there, pull your hair, stamp your feet, and cry, "Oh, poor, poor me!" without doing something to survive, would you? So with every challenge in life, face your problem and fight to survive it. Do your very best to deal with the problem in hand. If something you do does not make you or your situation any better, stop whatever that is (complaining would be one of them) and choose a better route to take. Be feisty!

3. Fight negativity with negativity. Your situation could be a lot worse. Imagine something worse than what you are going through now. Compare these situations—with which situation would you rather be dealing? Instead of breaking an arm, you could have broken a leg. Instead of losing a friend, you could have lost your entire family.

4. Fight negativity with positivity.

a) Think about something that you are grateful for, that makes you happy, that you love, and then replace your negative thought with the positive one.

Whenever I run into a stressful situation, I think about my Heavenly Father and my beloved earthly mother, and I become so grateful and happy to have them that I no longer find my situation so stressful; I am able to tolerate and endure the negativity so much better.

b) Determine the positive side of a negative situation. Sometimes, you cannot realize the positive side until some time has passed; it may not even appear until years after your ordeal. Remember the third exercise we did for "The Null of Negativity"?

5. Keep these points in mind as you face your obstacle:

a) There is always someone out there who is in a much worse situation than you, so be thankful for your own situation, that you are not going through something worse. Although you may be frustrated paying your bills, there are many who are homeless and would be glad to own the keys to your house. While you are complaining about having a bad hair day, at least one person on Earth is losing all of his or her hair receiving chemotherapy.

b) You are not suffering alone. Millions and millions of people are suffering this very minute, from the starved to the abused. And there may be people who are going through the same difficulty you are experiencing.

c) Everything passes, and so will your

current negative situation. When you are angry or upset, keep in mind that it will pass, so why waste your energy on something that will be gone tomorrow? It is true that a negative event in your life can affect your entire life, but there is nothing you can do when life throws stones at you. You simply have to prepare for any challenges and make the best of what you have. The tuberculin skin test I received when I was eleven months old caused the severe juvenile rheumatoid arthritis that will remain with me for the rest of my life. I know that life moves on no matter what happens to me, so it is best to move along with it and make the best of what I have. Would sulking and worrying about my life do me any good or turn my situation around?

6. Above all, keep your faith in God strong, and maintain that spiritual foundation. With the help from Jehovah's loving hands, you will be able to rise and overcome!

As you can see, you *can* be in control of what happens to you after a negative event. You do not need to be the victim of your troubles. Let your troubles be victims of your faith and positivity. If you do not let problems stop you, they cannot and will not stop you. Only you have the power to stop yourself. It is completely up to you—would you want to be stopped or unstoppable? I made my decision a long time ago. How would you like to join me?

Be Logically Sensitive, Stay Emotionless

Do you feel that you can make better decisions in the morning? Do you feel that your mind is clearer? Is it when you can logically think over an issue? Do you know why? Generally, in the morning, when we first get up, we are emotionless. As the day progresses, all of our emotions add up, and this is the reason why we tend to make rash decisions at night when our emotional level is at its highest. This is why it is important to think about something overnight without making a decision on an important thing right away. Usually, it is wise to decide on something after you have given some thought to it. In my own experience, I know how having a bit of time to think can be so crucial.

It is essential to deal with situations and issues without your feelings, positive or negative, and that includes dealing with positive situations, not just negative matters.

Since emotions can amplify a situation, good emotions can also negatively influence your decision-making process. For instance, let us say that your long-term crush popped the question after dating for a short while. You may feel so excited at first—it has always been your dream to marry this person, and now your dream has finally come true! Now put your giddy feelings aside. Sure, you may feel it is a good thing to tie the knot now, but is *right now* the right time? You have not known each other that long. If you are willing to risk an unhappy marriage or a divorce, then go for it.

Of course, I am not sending emotions down to the bottomless pit. After all, emotions are an important part of life, and they make up who we are as intelligent creatures. But emotions are powerful, so when you use them incorrectly, you risk negative outcomes. Emotions can drive us to do crazy things for love, sting others with hurtful and untrue words during arguments, commit crimes of passion, and spread terrible rumors because of hate and jealousy.

If you want to be mentally and logically sensitive during the decision-making process, stay away from emotions.

Below are three examples of dealing with a negative situation without involving your emotions.

Example I

You feel as though your world is falling apart when a friend has passed away. You cannot eat; you cannot sleep. All you can do is engulf yourself in your sorrow. You feel that you cannot live without your friend.

Put your emotions aside for a moment,

then examine the facts, which are:

a) Yes, your friend has passed away, but everyone must meet this end sooner or later.

b) You are able to *live* without your friend; of course, you will miss him or her immensely. Think about the time before you and your friend first met. You lived then without this friend, so it is not impossible to live without him or her now.

c) Life moves on; it is best to move along with it. Your friend would want you to move forward. Appreciate the time you and this friend were together; cherish the happy memories you built together.

Example II

When you lose your wallet, you feel as though you are doomed. You get upset after thinking all the negative aspects of the situation. But if you put your emotions aside, you will be able to think clearly. Yes, losing your wallet is unfortunate, but being upset about it will not bring it back to you. You have to think of ways to best limit any negative effects of your loss. If you cannot find your wallet, it will not be the end of your world.

Example III

My mother lost custody of me twice in America after disagreeing with doctors' recommended treatments — treatments that could have sent me to my grave. Both times, she did not let her own emotions trap her. She instead calmed down and focused on her problem to see how to solve it. She converted her initial anger (negative energy) into determination and courage (positive energy), so 1) she had no more of the negative energy and 2) she became even more motivated to fight and win.

My story about one of the terrifying custody cases my mother fought follows this chapter.

Through Maternal Love, Justice Prevails

A gold car, shimmering brightly under the ardent kiss of the morning sun, rolled into the driveway and slowly made its way to an empty parking space in front of Newington Children's Hospital. An Oriental woman got out of the car and opened the trunk. She took out a stroller, which she unfolded.

"Here again," a girl of seven, who clearly resembled the woman in her features, said under her breath. She looked at the building and inwardly wrinkled her nose. Hospitals were her least favorite places to visit, and yet, they were her home half of the time. After this visit in America, she and her mother would go to China for the fifth time to seek treatment of the severe juvenile rheumatoid arthritis that had made a home in her body since she was eleven months old. Her mother gave her an encouraging smile before locking the car doors.

"Shirley Cheng is here to see Dr. Zammit," the woman announced once they were inside the air-conditioned building.

"Okay, Juliet, he'll be right with you," came the reply.

The doctor soon appeared and told them to follow him. Both mother and daughter sensed something was amiss as they were led to a room. A smile was absent on his face, which was normally full of smiles.

He left them alone in the room, which held many officially dressed people whose expressionless faces turned to them. Minutes ticked by, yet none of the people moved or said a word. Their blank eyes burned into them.

The sickening feeling increased in Juliet. The date flashed into her mind: Friday, July 13, a Friday the 13th. *But that is a silly superstition, right?* she thought, wanting to dismiss it. But every time her eyes traveled back to the group of unmoving people, her disquietude grew.

The people continued to look at them attentively from their fixed places.

Shirley and her mother exchanged glances that seemed to spell out "What is going on?"

Dr. Zammit reappeared, still unsmiling. "Mrs. Cheng, do you want surgery for Shirley?" he asked.

"No," answered Juliet. "You need to fix the problem from the inside while fixing the outside, not just fixing the outside." He wanted to operate on six of Shirley's joints (her ankles, knees, and hips) when he did not even have any medication to effectively control her inflammation.

Taking one last look at Juliet, he turned and walked away. The crowd, as if on cue in a suspense movie, closed in on them.

"What is going on? What are you doing?

Did I lose custody again, just like what happened the first time?" questioned the stunned Juliet, referring to the custody case she fought against another doctor over treatment dispute when Shirley was only twenty-two months old. From the looks on their faces, her fear was confirmed.

A lady immediately pushed Shirley away from her mother to an adjoining room. Was Shirley afraid? Yes, but the feeling of anger invaded her being, flooding most of the space, leaving not much room for fright. What could she do? She could not speak English, only understand some. Even if she could speak, they were not here for reasoning. Their ears were not open to logic, nor their hearts to compassion and understanding.

Knowing the situation all too well, Shirley kept calm and composed. She colored in the coloring books the lady, whose position was unknown to her, provided. She knew if she broke down, it would make the situation worse. What the child did would be of importance on how they would judge the parent.

"I can't believe this! I made an appointment to see both Dr. Zammit and the eye doctor, but you just stop us from going back home." Juliet's body trembled with shock and fury. The doctor had called her to tell her that she could bring Shirley to see him and the eye doctor one last time before they left for China. Little did she know it was a trick. "We came here freely. If we didn't come here, you wouldn't have come to our home and held Shirley." Such a ruthless action! And it was supported by so many people, not just an action of one doctor.

Juliet knew she could win this case, just as she was victorious in the first, for she had grounds. She had the reasons, and because of this, she would regain custody—the right to be the parent of her own daughter. What she hated and feared most was the fact that this involved Shirley. If she were just fighting for herself, she would not worry—it would simply be fighting. What would she lose besides her life, which was so much less important than Shirley's? Now, since her daughter's life was on the line, it was so much more than just fighting; to her, the world was at stake. It was all about winning.

Shirley knew within her soul that her mother would defeat the battle between good and evil. She confidently looked at her mother as she was pushed away, down the hall and out of sight to the awaiting dungeon.

Days agonizingly passed in the hospital. Shirley's health steadily deteriorated. The doctor administered naproxen to her on an empty stomach, and did frequent x-rays and blood tests, at times, weekly.

Juliet was allowed to visit Shirley for only ten minutes, then later, for two hours. Afterward, she could stay with her daughter until eight at night. Finally, they extended the time to nine.

Once, before Juliet's visitation time limit

was extended to nine, Shirley had a high fever and wanted some ice cream. Juliet was feeding her the ice cream when she was ordered to leave immediately. It was two minutes past eight.

"Just let me finish feeding this to her and I'll leave," Juliet told the nurse. "I only have a bit left." She held out the four-ounce container.

"I'll call the police now," the nurse replied.

"Follow me," said the hospital security man, as he guided Juliet out. She saw police cars when she drove away.

***

During a court session, Dr. Zammit claimed, "The surgery is in Shirley's best interest," and that it was emergent. Juliet knew otherwise. The surgery was not emergent. It was not a life-threatening situation in which Shirley had to have the surgery in order to live. The surgery could be done at a later time when she would be able to withstand both the surgery itself and the recovery that would follow. It was not just the surgery that she would have to endure; she would have to go through extensive rehabilitation and therapy afterward. Moreover, the involved stress would severely compromise any good the surgery might do. Without commitment or long-term compliance, the likelihood of surgical failure and of reoccurring deformity would be great. Above all, how could Shirley have the surgery when the doctor did not even have any medicine to effectively control her current inflammation, not to mention the inevitable inflammation and complications that would follow the operation? This was not simply a life or death situation, Juliet knew; this was a paralyze or death situation, and the latter would be easiest on Shirley. She knew that without effective medicine to control Shirley's inflammation before and after the surgery, she would end up kissing her star goodbye or worse. So receiving the surgery at that time was unquestionably the worst option for Shirley, not the best, as the doctor had claimed.

"Your Honor, may I speak?" Juliet requested.

"No, you are not allowed," boomed the juvenile court judge. "Juliet Cheng, you are a seven-year child abuser!"

She ordered immediate surgery for Shirley. "If the child dies as a result of the surgery, you cannot sue the doctor," she said, looking straight into Juliet's eyes. "You can sue me."

The surgery was to be done on Tuesday.

Thinking fast, Juliet called up a doctor Shirley saw previously, and he recommended a pediatric rheumatologist, Dr. Athorn, in Philadelphia. "You have the right to a second opinion," he told her.

Thus, the surgery was postponed.

***

"I have received the report from Dr. Athorn. He recommended immediate surgery for Shirley," announced the judge.

Once again, the surgery was scheduled for Tuesday.

Juliet prayed with all her strength that her lawyer George Athanson—a former mayor of Hartford, Connecticut, for eleven years—could help. He was her new lawyer, as her previous lawyer could not help her.

On Sunday evening, George called ten judges to stop the surgery. Monday arrived without any news.

Juliet rushed to George's office that afternoon. "You must stop the surgery, you have to," she pleaded once she entered, towering over his desk.

"I just can't. I tried!" he barked.

Without waiting to hear what else he had to say, she drew money out of her pocket.

"Here." She put down one thousand dollars. "Stop the surgery."

Wordlessly, he buried his head in his hands. He could not stop the surgery even with all the money in the world. He was frustrated by it all. They needed a miracle. Juliet was drained. She knew that George was, too. He had been working on her case exclusively, putting all other cases aside. He and his assistants often stayed up in the office late at night, putting their heads together to get Shirley out of the confines of the hospital.

With a heavy heart, Juliet returned to her place and called the hospital to find out what time they would put the chisel into Shirley's soul.

"There's no surgery," Dr. Zammit told her.

"No surgery?" Juliet repeated. Did she hear him correctly?

"Yes, your lawyer canceled it. Didn't he tell you?"

Indeed, miracles do happen.

***

"I'm bringing the case to the federal court," George told Juliet. It was not going anywhere. Surgery had been blocked twice, as well as a full-body anesthesia test. How much longer could they keep this up? Juliet must win the custody case in order to save her pearl from a fate worse than death. There was no if's. Shirley was becoming all skin and bones and vomiting blood.

After the case was brought to the federal court, Juliet won a reprieve when the federal judge ordered an agreement between Juliet and the Department of Children and Youth Services:

In a two-month period, Juliet was to find a doctor to treat Shirley, following the treatment of her choice; the doctor must be a licensed medical practitioner, and the medical facility at which Shirley received treatment could be at any northeastern location, including Newington

Children's Hospital. At the same time, Shirley's legal guardian, appointed by the federal court, should find two doctors: an orthopedic surgeon and a pediatric rheumatologist. These three doctors in turn would determine whether Shirley needed the surgery. If two doctors stated that Shirley did not need surgery, there would not be any surgery for her. Otherwise, if two decided upon surgery, there would be one. After the two-month period, they would arrive at a decision on the statements made by the three doctors. The term would end on December 10, 1990.

When judgment day arrived, Juliet headed toward George's office to wait for the sentence. Juliet managed to pass all the reporters who were crowding outside the lawyer's office. She stepped into the tiny office, where George and two of his assistants, who were lawyers themselves, were found. They each had the same thought: whether Juliet had won the case. Would Shirley be in Juliet's arms once again, or would she forever be out of the reach of her loving mother? They would exert so much force to break the steel bond of the inseparable pair.

Suddenly, the door to the office opened, and in walked a very tired legal guardian. "Gosh!" he exclaimed, shaking his head. He had a hard time getting away from the mob outside. The reporters nearly ran him down. He looked at the four people before him. They searched for an answer in his eyes, but could not read anything from them. They held their breath.

"Well," he said, clearing his throat to add to the suspense, "would you want to know the whole story or the bottom line?"

"The bottom line!" all cried in unison.

The legal guardian walked toward Juliet, put out his hand, and patted her right shoulder. "You won, you won, Juliet."

Juliet nodded, her lips spreading into the widest smile her face had ever owned. Was she surprised? No. She always had faith that she would win. Her confidence had grown more so during the past two months of the trial. She had been praying, seeking support and guidance from the Almighty One. Yes, He had answered her prayers.

"But even if you did not win the case," the legal guardian continued, "no surgeon from any of the hospitals throughout Hartford, including this one, is willing to do the surgery for Shirley." The case had become international news, and the talk of many. The hospitals would not dare perform the surgery on Shirley even if Juliet lost the case. Juliet had many supporters, and it would have caused much trouble if they laid a single hand on Shirley when it was so strongly opposed.

One of the assistants, Steve, who always doubted her strong confidence of winning, went over to Juliet. "I believe you now," he said, shaking his head.

Juliet gave George a hug and a peck on the cheek.

"Hey, what about me?" asked Steve. Juliet gave him a hug and a peck, too.

Although the room was small, its happiness was radiating larger than the whole world. The celebration was not a loud one, but the expression on each face was more than any boisterous rejoicing could ever replace.

"So, do you have a back door?" inquired the legal guardian after handing George the three reports. Chuckling, George led him to the back door, where he could leave peacefully without getting trampled on.

The lobby was filled with reporters, each snapping shots around the place, while others held out microphones, hoping to catch something nice to air.

Into one microphone, Juliet simply said, "It's God's will."

Some of the names in the story have been changed to protect the individuals' privacy.

What's in It for Me?

How do you feel when someone says something very mean to you? I assume that you would feel hurt, angry, upset, and frustrated, all at once. You do not need to be told that this is a natural reaction; after all, it would be quite non-human for us not to have those emotions. But the question is: how long do you have those feelings? How long do you let those negative emotions rule over you?

For some people, holding on to these feelings helps them believe that they have control over their situation.

Are they really in control? No. Rather, their emotions are in control. Yes, when you have these feelings, these feelings control you, not the other way around. Holding on to these feelings does not enable you to control anything. When you harbor this negativity past a "healthy time," it is best to move on. If you cannot, the question to ask yourself is, "What's in it for me?"

What is in it for you to continually hold bad feelings? Do you get anything good out of it? Does it make you feel good? Does it make you happy? (I truly doubt that.) Would it change the situation? Would the offender learn a lesson from it?

Next time, when Ms. Snobby treats you

badly, and it angers you, ask yourself, "What's in it for me?" When you find nothing in it for you, it is time to say goodbye to anger. Never let negative emotions control you. You be in control!

I know it is, at times, much easier said than done. But I also know that it feels *so* much better to throw away the negative feelings so you will not miss out another minute of enjoying all the good feelings. So if you seriously desire to be in control, a bit of effort will greatly help you conquer negativity.

Personally, blocking out negativity is an essential part of my life. It makes me cringe to even think about what could have happened to me if I had not. What a total mess my life would have turned out! Not only am I blind and disabled, but I also have to endure daily discomforts, such as sleeping disorders, severe loss of appetite, and persistent sneezing and running nose, among others. I could be a very grumpy, depressed individual who sulks in her room all the time. But instead, I am a happy, positive person who actively writes all day in her room. Although the latter part stays the same (I am usually in my room), I am not ol' Scrooge! Which person would you rather be?

Are You Hungry Enough?

What directly affects your actions in life? It is your attitude: your opinion of the situation you are in, how you view what you are going through. For example, let us say you just broke up with someone you have been dating for two years, and you could either react positively or negatively. If you think, "Oh, this is not the end of my life; things could be a lot worse," you will not fall into any hole you might have otherwise created for yourself. On the other hand, if you say, "This is it! I'm unloved and I feel miserable," it will definitely throw you into a giant hole, and you will in turn feel unmotivated to move forward.

Being positive and remaining positive in negative situations can be easier said than done. How can you achieve positivity when you are in the dark? Get your deepest desires out!

Your desires should be the driving force in making you positive. Your desires are the fuel that get the vehicle—your attitude—going in the right direction. It all depends on your desires. If your desire for moving forward is strong enough, it will be able to conquer your negative feelings. For instance, when I lost my eyesight, my desires for a happy life defeated any feelings of sadness, frustration, or depression; those feelings did not even get a chance to show their ugly faces before my desires prevailed!

Why many people cannot seem to get out of their holes is that their desires are simply not strong enough. They may feel the desire to do something, but if they are not achieving a positive attitude, that tells me that their desires are still lacking. You absolutely have to hunger and thirst for happiness and moving forward. Just like a starving person in search of food, your desires have to propel you forward in search of the light at the end of the dark tunnel.

Use your desires to seek positivity on a daily basis. Positivity brings happiness, and it comes in all forms. You will feel good when you settle conflicts, make compromises, and conquer the cold shoulder. Many people cannot arrive at an agreement or end a conflict because they do not have the strong desire or willingness to do so. For instance, you have probably had lengthy arguments in which each party wants to be the winner. Their desire for being right overpowers their desire for ending the argument.

So your desires are everything! Only they will give you the attitude you need in order to take your giant steps forward. Always desire the desirable—the sweet, the pure, the beautiful—and it will lead you to a desirable life.

Go for Your Gold Medals in Life!

When people think about goals, some get frustrated. They feel that goals trap them. When they do not achieve their goals, they get disappointed, and become less motivated to establish goals in the future. They forget or do not realize the true meaning of goals. You make goals because you desire to accomplish something. Many goals give you a sense of purpose and direction. Without goals, you will not be clear what you want out of life.

Many people decide to live a goal-free life and accomplish things as they move along their journey. They set their lives on autopilot, going where ever their lives take them. They fall into a state of neutrality. Being neutral is being stuck, when you are not sending out any energy, neither positive nor negative. Being neutral does not bring you to anywhere meaningful. When you do not establish—or you abandon—your life's fundamental goals, you will not have the motivation to move forward, and you will lose your focus on what is truly important to you. You will not have energy or passion. You will only be existing, not living.

Is not life mostly about enjoying life? If you do not establish a sense of direction, of what you want out of life, you will not love the life you live.

Goals are not meant to be achieved one hundred percent of the time. Just as with any games you play, they are not meant for you to win all the time. Even after you lose, you will want to play again. Goals give you adventures in life. They provide even larger rewards when you achieve them. You cannot achieve everything in life, just as you cannot win every game you play. But the more you play, the more you will win. The more goals you make, the more achievements you will collect.

There is nothing wrong if you do not achieve your goals. If you have tried your best in something, that is all that matters. The best is all we can ask from anyone. It is important to know that to be successful does not necessarily mean that you should achieve a goal; it simply means that you have done your very best and have learned from what you did, right or wrong, along the way. Do not feel frustrated if you have not achieved what you have your heart set on; I think there is a right time for everything to happen, so if it has not happened yet, it may not be the right time.

What you learn from experience while you pursued your life's goals is what counts. Simply accomplishing goals without learning anything along the way holds not much value in itself. It is the lessons learned and the knowledge gained from experiences that matters.

Goals do not have to be large. They can be anything from taking some time to read a good book to helping a neighbor, or simply being a happy person.

Kinds of Goals

I categorize goals in mainly two groups: the dutiful goals and the passion goals.

Dutiful goals are the accomplishments you must complete in order to move forward, to live more comfortably for yourself and others. Cleaning the house, taking out the garbage, washing the dishes, sweeping the floor, and paying the bills, are all tasks you must complete. But it is necessary to set goals for all of these tasks. You should clean the house regularly, so you need to set your dutiful goal for performing cleaning regularly. Without setting dutiful goals, your tasks will pile up.

Passion goals are the desires of your heart, what your heart yearns to achieve. They are not necessary goals you need to achieve in order to survive; they are ones that will make your life much more enjoyable and valuable.

Some goals fall under both categories. Raising children, especially into good-natured and responsible adults, is a dutiful and passion goal, as are walking the dog and helping out someone in need.

Another name I give for goals, both the dutiful and passion ones, is "gold medals." I prefer calling them gold medals because when you achieve a medal, you feel honored and happy. When you achieve something in life that is meaningful, you will have fulfilled your purpose and sense of direction.

Achieve Your Gold Medals With...

A handful of ingredients are crucial to help you go for your gold medals in life.

Focus Stay focused. If you have a destination in mind, stick to it. If you want to drive to New York, would thinking about New Jersey help you get to New York? In order to get to New York, you have to focus on the necessary roads that will take you there.

Passion Passion is the reason that got you started with making your goal in the first place. It is your desire to want to achieve what your heart craves. Passion is the biggest motivator, besides your values. Remember, passion stems from your values and beliefs.

Having passionate feelings will make your actions seem effortless. The keyword is effortless. If you are trying too hard to get what you want—if you sweat too much, if you are sacrificing all the other good things you have in order to achieve this particular good thing—you will not achieve the fullest result of your goal. When you achieve it, you will be left tired, wasted, and might even feel that it was not worth your effort. Or you may give up altogether and abandon your goal halfway through. If you find yourself working way over your limits, you should then act upon another plan.

Commitment and determination
You need to commit to your goal and be determined to achieve it. You need one hundred percent commitment. Even with ninety-nine percent, you will eventually give up and abandon your pursuit.

Specification
The more specific you are with a goal, the more satisfied you will be once you have achieved your goal. Specification brings satisfaction.

If your goal deals with numbers, name a number. If you want to slim down fifteen pounds, make it your gold medal to lose fifteen pounds, not just "some." Because if you just say that you want to lose some weight, then when you lose five pounds, you may not feel completely happy. To be satisfied about what you have achieved, be specific about what you want.

Not all goals can be specific if the goals do not deal with numbers. For instance, your goal may be becoming a good teacher. The level of "good" depends on how good you want to be. The best way to establish such vague goals is to do your best. So if you want to be a good teacher, make it your goal to do your best in being a good teacher.

Fear no failure
Do not worry about failing. Do you sometimes start out fearing

failure even before you go after your goal? Then you find yourself erasing your heart's desires from your mind right after the goal first popped into your head, right? But do you know how reasonable is your fear? Is your fear the fear of physical injuries or is it the fear of humiliation? If it is the latter, ask yourself, "Is preventing humiliation more important than doing what I love?" How would you know you would be humiliated anyway? Remember, fear blocks rational thinking and reasoning, so it is best to discard your fears and worries, unless you have reasonable concerns. There is a difference between worry and concern, and you will read more about it in the following chapter.

The best winners in life are the best losers. If you can fail without being angry, and if you are able to stand back up, you are a true winner in life.

Open up to risks Having a daring spirit and being open to losses will allow you to keep your eyes open for new roads to explore and discover.

Positivity Above all, have an optimistic spirit.

I always urge others to go for their gold medals in life. But there are times when it is not such a good idea to do so. Do not make goals that will result in harm to others or for which you have to deal with dishonest people.

How Daring Are You?

Are you daring enough to enjoy life to its fullest? Do you take risks? I am referring to risks that could potentially change your life for the better.

It is important to take risks. Taking risks allows you to explore, discover, and learn new things; it brings you to a whole new road you have never before traveled. Without taking risks or seizing the opportunities to know new things, you would be stuck on one road for quite some time, missing out on new experiences you could truly enjoy. If you do not try something, how can you know that it will be impossible or that you will not enjoy it? You will never find out if you do not try.

Risks do not have to be risky at all, and many times, you will not view them as risks. For example, starting a new relationship is a "risk." You could get a broken heart as a result of entering into a relationship, but chances are, you could potentially find your soul mate, too.

Most things in life carry risks. Just living itself is risky. Whenever we get into our cars, we face roads to potential accidents. With every step we take, we could potentially trip and break a leg. With every bite of food we take, we have the potential to choke to death. But do we stop eating? Of course not, we have to eat in order to survive. Do we stop doing all of these things just because they involve risks? The reason we continue with these activities is that we need to move forward with life. Doing nothing can be risky as well, like simply lying in bed—the roof may fall on you, a car could careen into your house, lightning could electrocute you, and so on.

If you do not fear death, then what are you afraid of? Is death the final destination for everyone? No matter what you do or do not do in life, you will die. Is it not best to experience what life has to offer before your time ends? Is it better to risk to live than to simply exist?

Determine the risk factor of your goal: if your desires and pros outweigh the cons. In my situation, my goal is to get an eye surgery to restore my eyesight. My desire is to see this beautiful world again. I was an artist of the visual arts, so losing my eyesight is an immense loss for me. I absolutely want to get my eyesight back. The pros of a successful eye surgery include restoring my eyesight. The con of my goal is that if the surgery fails, I would not be able to see. The worst scenario would be that the surgery would permanently damage my eye. One eye doctor told me that I could lose the eye if the surgery did not go well. I am, however, determined to have the operation because the pros and my desires outweigh the risks. But I will first find the right eye surgeon. Without the right doctor, I will not have any surgery. So that goal of mine produces another goal: to find Dr.

Right. And that is the goal I must achieve first. Once I find the right surgeon, I am going to focus on the pros of my main goal and hope for the very best.

Learn from nature. The plants and animals have survived through elements of life and time. They have survived countless storms and hails, yet they are still thriving today and continually growing in abundance. The animals do not work; they do not make money and worry where they will find food or where they will dwell. All of their needs are supplied in fullness by life. Why can we not put our worries behind us? Would our worries help us in any way? Would our worries give us food, give us clothing, give us shelter?

One who frets over the future has not learned from the past. Think back to the earliest era of human existence. They had no electricity nor had they had any technology. And yet early humans had survived, and our species has survived and bloomed to this date. Can we not learn from their existence, our past, as well?

Concern and worry are not the same. Concern is productive; it still motivates you to focus on your problem and gives you the ability to think of ways to make your situation better or solve your problem in hand. It lets you be prepared for any challenges and difficulties you may face in a given situation, so you can take precautions. I am concerned about having the eye surgery because of the risks involved. Because I am concerned, however, I do not make my decision right away upon seeing one eye surgeon. I am going to see many eye doctors so that I might gather enough information to base my final decision on. I have also done some research on cataract extraction surgery as a result of being concerned. If, on the other hand, I only fret about my situation, I will not accomplish anything. I will only decide not to have the surgery. So worrying stops me; concern allows me to continually move forward, but with precaution and planning.

    Lastly, as you have probably already gathered, taking a risk does not mean you should jump into the water right away without thinking about it. I strongly recommend that you think over the pros and cons of your goal, and determine their weight.

Disable Your Disability

Just as it is essential to focus on your goal and block out negativity, it is important to be realistic and to understand your limitations. You cannot hide your limitations, but you can find another route to do what you want without having to encounter your limitations.

"Ultra-abled" is a term I coined when, one day, I suddenly had a new personal motto: "I'm not disabled—I'm ultra-abled!" An ultra-abled person is one who is not only able to overcome their limitations but also able to rise well above the average person. Healthy people can be disabled when they let negativity conquer them and allow obstacles hinder them from realizing and pursuing their life's dreams and passions.

The first step in overcoming a limitation you have is to accept it, if you cannot change it. The next chapter talks about how to accept or reject your mortality or limitation effectively.

I, for instance, lost my eyesight at the age of seventeen. Blindness is a limitation I have. That is a fact. I acknowledge my blindness; I do not say that it is not my limitation. Yet, I am able to find other avenues to explore. I no longer can draw or see the world around me with my eyes, but I am able to write to capture what I see with my heart.

Therefore, the next step in overcoming your limitation is to limit it. Limit its power and effects over you by focusing on what you are able to do, not what you are unable to do. If you sing beautifully, focus on your talents as a good singer, not on your weak areas. By focusing on your strong points or what other avenues you can explore, you will be able to limit your limitations or disable your disability.

Your heart will be your sole leader as it guides you to new avenues to explore and discover. Listen to it carefully, as I have, when it takes you to the two roads in life: the road to ability, which will lead you to happiness, strength, and success; and the road to disability, which will bring you only misery that glues you to the same spot. You know that you have the power to disable yourself or enable yourself, so which road will you choose?

When I lost my eyesight, I chose to be unstoppable. I did not want to make my situation worse than it was already. It is my life; I want to love the life I live, and it is up to me to fulfill that goal.

I have never given up in life, not after years of agonizing physical pain, moving from one hospital to another, and not even after going through the fright of nearly losing my mother forever. How could I let this obstacle stop me and hinder me from living a meaningful life?

Losing my eyesight does not mean I have lost my life, my vision; it just means that I will need to open other doors for other delights in life, and I have found plenty of doors to open.

The place to where my life has brought me after my eyesight kissed me goodbye was a total surprise to me: my destiny led me in the direction of a professional writing career, as though someone had decided to rewrite the script of my life on the spur of the moment, adding more twists and turns to the plot (as if my life had not already had enough drama!). But I would have to salute the Author of my life: God; thanks to my blindness, I have become a published author, poet, and a motivational speaker, giving me the opportunity to expand my horizon and allowing me to touch more people to bring humor, hope, and healing.

The decision was up to me to either move along with life or not, and I have chosen to waltz along with it. Although I am blind, I can see far and wide, as my dancing heart tells me all that it sees.

No way will I ever let life's mountains block me from reaching the path of true happiness. Life took away my eyesight, I brought forth a new vision.

Acceptance or Rejection?

In order to accept and reject your mortality or a limitation you have, you need to:

1. Determine your desires. What do you want? How do you want to be?

2. Identify your values and beliefs. What values are important to you? What qualities do you want to have or be associated with? The decisions and judgments you make in life will be based on your values and beliefs.

3. Determine whether your quality is changeable. Would you be able to alter the subject in question without causing you any harm, without too much difficulty? Can it be done effectively? Would you be happy with the change?

Keep in mind that

1. It is best to accept your quality if you cannot change it. You are born the way you are; you are given the life you live.

2. You can effectively reject your quality only when you are able to change the subject in question to something better for you, to something more desirable. Otherwise, simply rejecting your quality will only cause resentment. You will not like your situation, and that is going to stick with you for a long time,

like a piece of gum stuck to your shoe, until you learn to accept it. What good would rejection do you? It will not make your situation better; it will only make it worse, so it is definitely not what you want to do for yourself. You deserve better than that!

As you go about overcoming your limitation or changing your undesirable quality to something desirable, you need to hold on tightly to your spiritual foundation. It will help you while you accept or reject your mortality. Many times, you must put effort in what you do. Changing something you do not like about yourself can be difficult. Be patient and do your best. As long as you are truly serious about achieving what you want, you will most likely accomplish it.

My personal example:
The fact is I am disabled with severe juvenile rheumatoid arthritis, so I endure physical pain, stiffness, and limited mobility, and I have to depend on someone to care for me. That is a quality I possess.

I go through the three steps to see if I should accept or reject my disability.

1. I determined that I want to be healthy. I want to be pain-free, I want to be able to walk and take care of myself. Above all, I want to be happy.

2. My value is to be a happy person, enjoy life to its fullest, and make the most of my situation.

3. I understand that I cannot change my disability; I cannot make it disappear into thin air, so it is in turn, unchangeable.

I decided to accept my disability. My values and common sense override my desires to be disease-free, and yet, I am still achieving my desires to be happy.

I accept my disability, but that does not mean that I have given up. I simply acknowledge that I do have the disease, and that it is important to move on and fulfill my values and beliefs — to be a happy person, enjoy life, and make the most of my situation.

If I reject it when I cannot change the fact that I am disabled, I will be miserable with myself. I would not like the situation I am in. So what good will that do me? It will not change my situation, only make it worse.

Win with Positivity

They say that the way to a man's heart is food. Well, the way to success is positivity. The steps are quite simple, and most of the time, it can be done effortlessly.

You need to perform three steps—think, feel, and act—in a positive way in order to attract positive energy to achieve your heart's desires.

Here is a rundown of the steps.

1. Think about your goal. Why is it important for you to achieve it? What additional good things you want to come out of it? What are the benefits you will receive when you accomplish your goal?

It is important to first concentrate on your desires, what you want to achieve or do. You then should think over the pros and cons for achieving your goal, and decide whether the good outweighs the bad. If the good overrides the bad, go for it, and focus on your goal in hand and put the bad aspects aside. Thinking about the cons is a good step to take in the beginning; it lets you prepare for any main challenges you may face, so you will not be too surprised when you do run into any unpleasant situations. But once their purpose is served, do not focus on the bad aspects anymore. Otherwise, negative thoughts will only make you less enthusiastic about achieving your goal and will make you more doubtful of your goal.

Visualization plays a vital role in the thinking step. Generally speaking, most sighted people and those who were previously sighted, like yours truly, think with pictures. Many have thoughts accompanied by images. When you hear or read a description, like in a book, your mind will automatically provide you with images. If you read "A red rose kissed by the moonlight," you will imagine such a scene. If I say a ballerina pink elephant, you will see a pink elephant dancing in your mind's eye. You may know Brian Hyland's song, "Itsy Bitsy Teenie Weenie Yellow Polka-Dot Bikini." When you hear it, an image of an itsy-bitsy-teenie-weenie-yellow-polka-dot bikini will pop up into your head. That is why writers show without telling. They let readers do the imagining and the feeling.

When you think about your goal, picture it as well. This is something you will most likely do unconsciously, without needing to be instructed anyway.

Visualization gets your emotions going stronger more than simply thinking about something. If you can see it in your mind's eye about your desired outcome, you will be able to spiritually experience it. It will make your desired outcome feel more tangible, as though you can almost touch it, and that can really be a huge motivator.

2. Thinking about all of the benefits your

achieved goal can bring will get your emotions fired up. Since emotions are powerful motivators in any situation, having strong and unwavering feelings about your goal is a crucial step. You will get excited about all the benefits, and all the possibilities that you will be better in different ways. You will feel impatient to get started.

3. Those feelings and emotions will lead you to act. Let those feelings be the motivators of your action. If you only think about your goal and feel excited about it, it will not get you anywhere. You will not achieve anything without acting upon your plans. If you sit in a car, think about your destination and get excited about what you will do there, and yet you do not involve some locomotion—if you do not start the engine and drive—that car will not magically fly you there. You must act, act, act. If I only think about seeing again and feeling excited about it, without visiting any eye surgeons, I would not achieve anything.

Okay, so you already know all that. But as with anything in life, you need to know the trick to think, feel, and act in a certain way to accomplish what you want. Perform all the steps in a positive way.

The mind does the thinking, the spirit does the feeling, and the body does the acting. There needs to be good communication between all three of these systems, and they need to receive the same message from you, in order to give you what you desire fully. If they receive mixed directions, they will be confused to as what you actually want to achieve. So provide them with the same directions, the same vibe, and the same energy.

When you positively think about your goal, positively picture it. Do not think one way and picture it another way. It is perfectly fine if you need to think out the pros and cons of a situation — which I actually recommend that you do — but do not mix positive images and negative images together with positive thoughts and negative thoughts. Match them so you are staying in clear focus. If you think in a positive way and you imagine it in a negative way, you will not be in focus and clearly know what you want and do not want; the pros and cons of your goal will not be clear enough to you. It will be confusing to your systems, so you will have conflicting feelings and emotions.

Having opposite thoughts and feelings at the same time, occupying the same space, will only cause chaos in your spirit; therefore, your body will not take the correct action. No two opposite energies are capable of sharing the same space at the same time. If you mix two solutions of colored water in one container, the colors will mix, thus not giving you their purest forms, and they will take up twice the space needed for one solution. So if you have both negativity and positivity, you will get mixed results, not the ultimate outcome you want to achieve. You will not receive the best, the fullest, the complete result you desire.

Here is an example where thinking, feeling, and acting are performed in a positive way:

Julie wants to lose ten pounds for the summer season. She wants to sunbathe in the latest trend of bikini—a bright pink one she has had her eyes on for a while—at the beach. Please note that I said "ten pounds," not just "some weight." Remember, be as specific about your goal as possible.

She thinks about her goal. She thinks that she will feel healthier, be healthier, and be less likely of having diabetes, heart problems, and hypertension. Not only will she look better and more attractive, but she also will feel more energetic and confident. She may even find a new boyfriend.

While thinking about all the benefits, Julie starts getting very excited. She starts picturing herself in that hot pink bikini, turning heads wherever she goes. She feels energetic already! She starts feeling impatient to get started with a good weight-loss program.

Julie begins to act. She continually thinks and feels positively, so her actions match her thoughts and emotions. After a month of exercise and eating right, she has become ten pounds slimmer. Her effort has been awarded when she catches the eye of a gentleman when sunbathing at the beach in the bright pink bikini.

What if Julie had sent out mixed signals to her mind, body, and spirit? Instead of having positive thoughts, feelings, and actions, she had both positivity and negativity.

This is one example of this happening:

While Julie was thinking about the benefits of becoming slimmer for the summer, she starts having doubts. Her vision of a slimmer Julie turns into a ten-pound chocolate cake, her favorite dessert. She feels sad about having to sacrifice the cake to get what she wants. She winces when she thinks about the workout she needs to complete. And does she even have the time to exercise? She is bombarded with one negative thought after another. She does not feel as excited about her goal as before. In the end, she abandons her goal altogether.

Last Few Words

Everyone travels down his or her own life road but will eventually arrive at the same destination. Everyone has a common goal in life, and that is to die happy. If they could nod with approval as they look back on their lives, they would know they have achieved their fundamental goals. Sure, there have been ups and downs, and they have made mistakes here and there, but as long as they know that they have done their best with living, that will make them happy, and they will have thus fulfilled their life's purpose and goals.

While you are on Earth, put your energy into good use. God gives us free will, so use that free will wisely. He allows us to do what we want and to make our own rules and laws. So it is obvious that we have the power and ability to make a difference in our lives. Go make that positive difference, one kind act at a time.

Put your best effort in everything you do in every situation. No matter what position you are in—as a parent, as a student, as a daughter—do your best in being your best. Always make the most of your situation, of your means. If you have got only a fork and a spoon, make the most of them. Use the fork as a back scratcher or to comb your hair. Use the spoon to play music. Hey, some people may not even have a spoon and a fork.

Use your spiritual foundation to make a difference to your life, to someone else's life. And when everyone does that, the world will experience a domino effect. Remember those dance steps!

Life plays such blissful tunes, so open up your heart to welcome those melodies into your soul. Sing and rejoice over the beauties of our treasures; love and celebrate the joys of loving Jehovah and Jesus Christ to dance with your heart to the music of life! Soar with ultra-ability!

Spotlight Reviews
Excerpted Raves

If there is ever to be a poster person for people with ultra-abilities, it would have to be twenty-four-year-old Shirley Cheng. The author has turned her disabilities into an ultra-ability and written the awe-inspiring *Embrace Ultra-Ability!* Cheng's slim but power-packed motivational guide delivers what it promises with its wisdom, insights, and motivation. It is a volume to be read, re-read, and treasured for its originality, readability, and courageous approach to dealing with life's adversities, and from an individual who has had far more than her fair share of them.

Cheng is a first-class role model for taking the cards one is dealt in life and turning them into a winning hand. With clinical objectivity and without a sniffle of self-pity she describes the setbacks she suffered at eleven months of age when she contracted severe juvenile rheumatoid arthritis and later when she became fully blind at age seventeen. The story of how she overcame these disabilities as well as several misdiagnoses by medical practitioners, other attempts by legal authorities to rip her from her single mother's custody, and a delayed start in her formal education, is an inspiration for all readers—sighted, blind, abled or ultra-abled. Among Cheng's achievements are several books she has authored, edited, and designed, including a work co-authored with self-help icons such as Wayne Dyer, Tony Robbins, and Brian Tracy. She also does motivational tours and runs her own Web site.

Cheng's basic philosophy is, "If I have succeeded, so can you." She lays out in detail the guidelines to follow and the criteria to observe to obtain spiritual fulfillment, happiness, love, and respect, among other benefits. She stresses, however, that it is the reader who must take ultimate responsibility for his or her own physical, mental, emotional, and spiritual well-being. With typical humility she refers to her volume as only a basic guidebook. But it is a guidebook full of sage advice, helpful exercises, common sense analyses, and tough love prescriptions in chapters such as, "Go For Your Gold Medals in Life," memorable anecdotes from her life experiences, and two more detailed stories, one about her own birth, the other about her mother's custody battle to keep her, that are gems of classic storytelling. The latter is also frightening because of what could have happened if Mrs. Cheng had not been able to stave off the misdiagnosed medical procedures with which her daughter was threatened. It seems that bravery and persistence are common threads with the Cheng women.

The author's attitude toward life's obstacles is perhaps best summed up in the following quotation from her chapter, "Always a Tomorrow," about everyone's need for hope.

It is a mantra well suited for others to follow too:

"No mountain is high enough to hold me back; no wind is strong enough to blow me down. There are stars I must reach; there are roads I must take, and with my blooming hope inside, I spread my wings wide to embrace all that tomorrow will bring."
— M. Wayne Cunningham
ForeWord CLARION Reviews   Perfect 5-Star Rating

In a society that is self absorbed, unjustly critical and judgmental; out comes an honest and humble perspective from a young, prophetic muse, whose inner perception is astounding.

Embrace Ultra-Ability! defines the very essence that truly needs to exist in all of us. We have no place for pity within our lives after reading about the determination, resilience and extreme faith Shirley holds towards her life and her experience. The courage to share her understanding in anticipation others will follow is a sheer sign of true leadership and accountability.

And as a matter of fact, each teenager should be given this book in High School as a basis from which to build their values, morals and gratitude toward life.

With what we view as set-backs, Ms. Cheng views her challenges as monuments of growth and turns them in to the highest of accomplishments and achievements.

I honor her endurance and envy her strength.
— *Trish Lay, Life Coach, Speaker*
Founder of Souls at Play Productions

Embrace Ultra-Ability! is a powerful book that demonstrates a spiritual insight I have not seen in a person as young as she is. By skillfully intertwining her spiritual insights with her personal story, she is able to explain how every one has the ability to enjoy a happy, loving and prosperous life full of rich rewarding journeys. I highly recommend this book for those seeking ways to embrace every aspect of their lives and develop them to serve others.
— *Rowena Holloway, Ordained Lay Minister, Speaker*

(*Embrace Ultra-Ability!*) is filled with wise, practical, and eminently usable advice and guidance that can be utilized as a whole, or in discrete segments, depending upon the reader's needs and situation. Everything Shirley talks about has a backdrop of deep spirituality and strong ethics...here is a person who works every hour of every day to practice her faith, to celebrate her blessings, and to constantly resist falling into self-pity or bitterness. This is an inspiring book and can be used daily by most readers to keep their spirits uplifted and their love of life, reinforced!
— *Dr. Paul A. Johnson, Ph.D.*
Clinical & Consulting Psychologist

I was impressed with the scope of this material. Cheng manages to do a more than credible job of addressing nearly every roadblock to personal success, in fact, she clearly defines core issues and gives steps to surround them and successfully incorporate them into our beingness. Her candor and honesty allow us to see ourselves in all our humanity and majesty, accepting, pushing forward two steps, one step back, enjoying, rejoicing for the chance and the chances, always more chances.

I recommend this book to conscious people in the act of living the best life possible.
— *Patricia Hamilton, Publisher, Park Place Publications*

Motivational speaker and poet Cheng offers a heartfelt guide to building the foundations for a good life.

Cheng has had her share of miseries: A crippling case of juvenile rheumatoid arthritis, which was not only excruciatingly painful but kept her from school and almost sent her into foster care, was followed by the loss of her vision at the age of 17. So if she chooses to live in happiness, then her tools to achieve that state certainly have fashioned one shining example. Cheng is a forceful believer in God Almighty. But readers need not be believers to find the everyday wisdom in her life purposes: to be a good person with good intentions and to enjoy life to its last sensuous, joyous morsel.

Writing with verve and conviction, and ever cutting to the chase, she covers the ingredients of the foundation...she provides working examples of how to handle the negativities that enter life...moving beyond simply tendering good words.

Cheng could easily have become sad and bad, but good and happy is her path. These lifeways were her ticket to the high road.
— *Kirkus Discoveries*

Embrace Ultra-Ability! is an excellent and effectively written book by Shirley Cheng. You will feel your mind open to her insightful thoughts, spiritualism and advice, while at the same time find yourself reaching ultimate goals such as inner peace, self-acceptance and happiness.

Embrace Ultra-Ability! is a key that will enable you the reader, to finally unlock doors that have blocked you from understanding and really seeing what is beyond your own impaired vision.

This book is very effective and empowering in teaching positive affirmations, self-confidence, self-love and true sight. A must for every reader!

Through Shirley Cheng's book, you will gain the strength needed to reach your ultimate goal in life of a true balance.
— *Dorothy Lafrinere, WomensSelfEsteem.com*

Shirley Cheng's vibrant prose refreshes the soul. Her positive message of hope and love has universal appeal. In *Embrace Ultra-Ability* she writes about her appreciation of life, shares her insights and captures beauty in every moment. To Shirley, life is an adventure filled with possibility.

Reading *Embrace Ultra-Ability* is a positive experience that will lead you to a better life. Shirley Cheng's unique view of the world and encouraging words help you to see life from a different perspective.

As Shirley introduces her ideas she also talks about her own struggles and accomplishments. By embracing a life of purpose she shows the way to a much more positive lifestyle.

— *The Rebecca Review, Top Ten Amazon.com Reviewer*

"This small book is simply a tender nudge," writes Shirley Cheng in the opening chapter of this joyful volume that combines the basics of faith and positive thinking into a gentle guide that's well-illustrated by the author's experience.

Cheng's own journey as a blind and physically disabled award-winning author serves as a unifying inspiration throughout the book.

She enthusiastically urges us forward, step by positive step, toward becoming "Ultra-Abled."

—*Malcolm R. Campbell, Campbell Editorial Services*

Need words of wisdom, something profound? Prepare to be surprised at the insightfulness which comes from an unexpected place. Shirley Cheng's recommendations will motivate and impress you. Her thoughts will challenge you to question and rethink your assumptions, and she'll offer an elusive yet meaningful alternative order to the dubious skepticism you carry around.

Shirley will humble you as she displays her philosophy for a happy existence.

Through her optimism and wise outlook, you will find hope. In spite of the fact that Shirley has suffered her whole twenty-four years of life, she describes herself as ultra-abled.

Find zeal for life's quests and embrace your ultra-abilities. As you open your mind, you'll be challenged to be the best you can be, and reminded of life's enchantments. Recommended for anyone who needs a lift to the brighter side of life.
— Christina Francine, CFrancine@mail2world.com
Reviewer's Bookwatch, Midwest Book Review

Adopting Shirley's positive views on living and using some of her suggested techniques can bring the same resolute strength into your life with wonderful results. A timeless and ageless fountain of hope that can be read over and over.
— *Robbie Miles, Brush Artist and Teacher*

About the Author

Shirley Cheng, born in 1983, a blind and physically disabled award-winning author (with fifteen awards), motivational speaker, self-empowerment expert, poet, author of seven books and contributor to ten as of 2007, is a miracle survivor with tremendous talents, an exceptionally tenacious spirit, and a colorful personality. She was diagnosed with severe juvenile rheumatoid arthritis at only eleven months old. She spent her early years in constant pain, confined to a wheelchair, and was hospitalized for many years while living between China and America until 1994. Unable to receive any form of education until her health was stabilized, Shirley started attending school at age eleven in a special education class in elementary school. Back then, she knew very little English, and her knowledge on other subjects was non-existent. Miraculously, she mastered grade level in all areas after approximately 180 days of attendance, and she immediately entered a regular sixth grade class in middle school.

Shirley has a voracious appetite for books, reading an average of six hundred pages (three books) daily, and has read over a total of two thousand books. Since sixth grade, she has received 100 on every NYS essay test, and stayed at the top of the class ever since. She was awarded for achieving the highest grade of 97 in

Earth science in her eighth grade class. She was the Student of the Year and the Student of the Month, as well as a three-time winner of the National Reflections Program in visual arts. She has a passion for writing both prose and poetry. One of her short stories, *Mary Miller, the Elusive Lady*, received Honorable Mention and was published by the *Poughkeepsie Journal* in 1997, and her poem, *The Colors of the Rainbow*, earned merit status and was published in *Celebrate! New York Young Poets Speak Out* in 1999.

Shirley was a contributor to her high school newspaper, providing artwork in tenth grade. She received a standing ovation when she delivered a speech as a candidate for student body vice president in ninth grade.

When her eyesight began to deteriorate at the beginning of tenth grade, she had to use two magnifying glasses, holding one on top of the other, on enlarged print to do her work throughout the year, including the artwork she provided for the school newspaper. In classes, she learned only by listening to her teachers, even with chemistry and math, as she was unable to see the blackboard; still she maintained excellent grades.

Unfortunately, Shirley completely lost her vision in April of tenth grade. She then received home-tutoring, and successfully completed all her schoolwork by using cassette tapes and tape recorders. She wrote and balanced long chemistry formulas and equations without vision or Braille (she cannot use Braille because of her severe arthritis). Her high school overall average was 97 (a 3.9 GPA without any advanced placement classes). But Shirley could not accumulate enough credits to receive a high school diploma from her school due to her vision loss. In 2002, she received her high school equivalency diploma. She took the entire GED test, including mathematical calculations, graphs, and an essay, in her head, and received a special recognition award for scoring an exceptionally high 3280. She was a student speaker at the GED graduation ceremony, and received a standing ovation for her speech.

Shirley became an author at age twenty, completing three books within one year. She wrote her books using a screen reader on her computer, typing with her two index fingers at the speed of about sixty words per minute. She successfully completed every self-publishing task, including formatting her manuscripts, on her own.

In January 2006, Shirley tied for first place in Be the Star You Are! Second Annual Essay Contest founded by New York Times bestselling author, TV/radio personality Cynthia Brian, garnering her a third appearance on Cynthia's live radio show. Shirley's winning entry, titled *The Jewel from Heavenly Father*, is dedicated to her beloved mother Juliet Cheng. In the following January, Shirley won Honorable Mention in the same contest for her essay, *I Hold the Power*, her personal story of overcoming blindness at the age of seventeen. In

January 2008, Shirley was yet again one of the winners in the contest, earning Honorable Mention for her essay, *My Mother: A Fighter, a Victor, a Lover*, which applauds her stellar mother for being a courageous and loving fighter to protect her life at all costs.

Shirley has an immense passion for life and is full of life and vigor. Despite her severe disabilities, Shirley has striven to overcome overwhelming obstacles and she is living the life she loves, while she empowers, inspires, and motivates others to do the same.

Shirley was brought up in a very simple, single-parent, Chinese-speaking family with no influence on education. She pursues her education on her own. She has extraordinary goals with the aspiration of attending college at Harvard University, where she plans to earn doctorates in microbiology, zoology, astronomy, physiology, and pathology, after a successful eye surgery.

Shirley is a true magical gift, a star with endless shine. She is "the blind" who sees far and wide.

Shirley As an Advocate

Shirley is also an advocate of parental rights in children's medical care, and aide/caregiver monitoring and screening for students with special needs and disabled people.

As a parental rights advocate, she wants to help today's loving parents protect and keep custody of their children. "In America, parents risk losing custody of their children forever if they disagree with doctors' recommended treatments, or even when they want a second opinion," says Shirley, a survivor of two custody battles her mother Juliet Cheng had with doctors. Shirley adds, "When doctors ask yes or no, parents should have the right to say no."

Shirley's last case made international headlines in 1990; Juliet appeared on *CBS This Morning* with Paula Zahn as she fought to save Shirley's life and prevent her from receiving the harmful treatment recommended by her doctor in Connecticut.

Shirley promotes aide advocacy for the disabled because she was mistreated and abused by one-on-one aides when she attended school. "The trouble with uncaring aides actually lies with the authorities," she says. "If they had listened to my complaints and kept a close watch on the aides, I wouldn't have gone through all the suffering."

Other Books by Shirley

Shirley is also the author of:
- *Daring Quests of Mystics*
ISBN: 978-1-4116-5664-2
- *The Revelation of a Star's Endless Shine: A Young Woman's Autobiography of 20-Year Victories over Victimization*
(with foreword by Cynthia Brian)
ISBN: 978-0-6151-5044-4
- *Dance with Your Heart: Tales and Poems That the Heart Tells*
This book is available in Vietnam, published by the Women Publishing House in 2008 and translated into Vietnamese by Nguyen Bich Lan.
ISBN: 978-1-4116-1858-9
- *Waking Spirit: Prose & Poems the Spirit Sings*
(with foreword by New York Times bestselling author Cynthia Brian)
This book is a multi-award winner. The awards include Mom's Choice Awards, The Avatar Award for Spiritual Excellence in Literature (2008), best book in three categories of Reader Views 2007 Annual Literary Awards: First Place in Poetry Nonfiction, and Second Place in both New Age Nonfiction and Spirituality/Inspiration; award-winning finalist in the national Indie Excellence 2007 Book Awards, Honorable Mention in the 2007 New York Book Festival Competition, as well as Honorable Mention in 2007 DIY Book Festival.
ISBN: 978-0-6151-3680-6 (trade paperback)
978-0-6151-3893-0 (hardback)

- *Parental Rights in Children's Medical Care: Where Is Our Freedom to Say No? A Look at the Injustice of the American Medical System*
ISBN: 978-0-6151-4994-3
- *The Adventures of a Blind and Disabled Award-Winning Author: Inspiration & Motivation to Empower You to Go for Your Own Gold Medals*
The sequel to *The Revelation of a Star's Endless Shine*.
ISBN: 978-0-6151-7515-7

With highly acclaimed experts, including Dr. Wayne Dyer, Tony Robbins, and Brian Tracy, Shirley co-authored *Wake Up...Live the Life You Love: Finding Life's Passion* (ISBN: 978-1-9330-6305-8) in the bestselling *Wake Up...Live the Life You Love series*; she is also the co-author of *101 Great Ways to Improve Your Life, Volume 2* (ISBN: 978-0-9745-6727-3), along with leading experts, like Jack Canfield, John Gray, Richard Carlson, Alan Cohen, Bob Proctor, et al.

Shirley on the WWW

Visit Shirley on the Web at http://www.shirleycheng.com to learn more about her, her books, listen to some of her radio show interviews, e-mail her, and subscribe to her monthly newsletter, *Inspiration from a Blind*, to receive words of inspiration, special news and events information, and exclusive offers for members. Her newsletter issues are archived on her blog, http://blog.shirleycheng.com to which people can subscribe via e-mail or RSS.

Personalized autographed copies of all of Shirley's books are available from her website.

Her books are also available through Ingram, from Amazon.com (and their international sites) and BN.com, and also available through brick-and-mortar Waldenbooks and Borders stores.

Shirley is available for interviews, speaking engagements, book signings, and inspirational events.

www.ingramcontent.com/pod-product-compliance
Lightning Source LLC
LaVergne TN
LVHW011420080426
835512LV00005B/171